Books by Anita Borghese

The Down to Earth Cookbook

The Complete Book of Indonesian Cooking (coauthor)

Foods from Harvest Festivals and Folk Fairs

The International Cookie Jar Cookbook

Just Desserts

 *Foods from Harvest Festivals and Folk Fairs*

drawings by YAROSLAVA MILLS

FOODS from HARVEST FESTIVALS and FOLK FAIRS

The Best Recipes from and a Guide to Food Happenings Across the Nation

by Anita Borghese

Thomas Y. Crowell Company   Established 1834   New York

Designed by Joy Chu

Manufactured in the United States of America

Library of Congress Cataloging in Publication Data

Borghese, Anita.

Foods from harvest festivals and folk fairs.

Includes index.
1. Cookery, American.   2. Cookery, International.
I. Title.
TX715.B7255   641.5'973   77-968
ISBN 0-690-01655-7

10   9   8   7   6   5   4   3   2   1

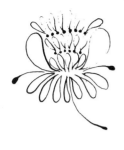

To Mother,
for her tenacity,
spirit, and devotion

Contents

Acknowledgments

My sincere thanks to the many people whose names appear below or throughout the book who have been so generous with their sharing of information or recipes that have made the book possible, and to the many people whose names, for varying reasons, do not appear but who have been equally generous and helpful.

Mrs. Judy Gadbois, Mrs. Louise Mutschler, and the Apple Festival Committee of Salem, Connecticut; Mr. Tom Perry, president, Apple Festival, Jackson, Ohio; Ms. Marlene F. Collins, secretary, the Geauga County Historical Society, Burton, Ohio; Mrs. Evelyn A. Walther, Elko Basque Club, Elko, Nevada; Ms. Pat Mroczek, Chamber of Commerce, Mr. Charles Kern of Kern's Sausages, Frankenmuth, Michigan; Mr. Mike Hofer and Mrs. Lucille E. Moles of the Biblesta Committee, Humboldt, Kansas; Mrs. Marion Warnock, president, and Miss Joan Matvieshen, secretary, of Canada's National Ukrainian Festival, Mrs. Yaroslava Mills and Mr. Myron and Mrs. Magda Surmach of West Nyack, New York, and Mrs. Halia Sluzar of Mississauga, Ontario; Mr. Frederick A. Shaw, manager, Chamber of Commerce, Holtville, California; Mrs. Dorothy L. Walkmeyer, executive manager, National Cherry Festival, Traverse City, Michigan; Mrs. Allegani Jani Schoffield Mc-Cullough of Stonewall, Texas, and Mrs. Ann Fowler Kennedy of Austin, Texas; Mrs. Patricia LaLand, Press Bureau, Colonial Williamsburg Foundation, Williamsburg, Virginia; Mrs. Alice Speck, chairman, Junior Baking Contest, Association of Connecticut Fairs, Mr. Robert Goldman, Connecticut Department of Agriculture, and Mr. Charles Norwood, Connecticut Department of Commerce; Mrs. Cora Tarnow, Danish Days Committee, Solvang, California; Mr. Bob Maxwell, publicity director, National Date Festival, and Mr. Robert B. Allen, Chamber of Commerce, Indio, California; Ms. Corrinne Lauterback, chairman, Duluth Folk Festival, Duluth, Minnesota; Father Marion of Most Precious Blood Friary, and Mr. Alfred Lepore, president, Ferrara Food and Confectionery Company, New York, New York; Ms. Barbara Beauchamp, program coordinator, Stephen Foster Center, White Springs, Florida; Mrs. Sarah Greensfelder, Mohawk Nation, via Rooseveltown, New York, Mr. Nicholas Schoumatoff, Trailside Museum, Ward Pound Ridge Reservation, Pound Ridge, New York, Mrs. Louella Derrick, Nedrow, New York, and Mr. Clifford Hall, Lafayette, New York; Mr. Kalani Cockett, Jr., and Ms. Susan Sunderland, Hawaii Visitors Bureau, Honolulu, Hawaii; Mrs. Margaret Voskuil, Board of Directors, Holland Guild Gezelschap, Cedar Grove, Wisconsin; Messrs. Bill Fisher and Jerry R. Coughlon of the Iowa State Fair, Senator John C. Culver of Iowa, Mr. Harold Mindermann of the Iowa Farm Bureau Federation, and Mr. Bill Gebhart of Gold Medal Products Company, Cincinnati, Ohio; Mrs. Romona Gautreau, executive director, Chamber of Commerce, Gonzales, Louisiana; Mr. Glenn Malone, secretary-treasurer, Chamber of Commerce, Montgomery, Minnesota; Mrs. Scottie Stowell, Chamber of Commerce, and Mrs. Ivy W. Dowd, *The Courier-Gazette,* Rockland, Maine; Ms. Sally Ann

Anderson, executive secretary–treasurer, Maple Festival, Jefferson, New York; Mr. John T. Powell, executive director, National Peanut Festival Association, Dothan, Alabama, and Mr. Lou King of the Alabama Peanut Producers Association; Mrs. Peg Zecher, Press Office, Kutztown Folk Festival, Swarthmore, Pennsylvania; The Honorable Jerry L. Hancock, mayor, Mrs. Dymple Green, chairman, Persimmon Pudding Contest, and Mr. Dana Dunbar, chairman, Persimmon Festival, Mitchell, Indiana; Mr. Charles Cubelic, director, Pittsburgh Folk Festival, Pittsburgh, Pennsylvania; Ms. Pauline T. Putnam, secretary, and Ms. Dorothy Hannigan, executive director, Chamber of Commerce Potato Feast Committee, Houlton, Maine, and Mrs. Jackie Tremblay, secretary, Chamber of Commerce, Fort Fairfield, Maine; Ms. Michele Morrison and Mr. Ned Harden, Pumpkin Show, Inc., Circleville, Ohio; Mr. Bill Williams, general chairman, International Rice Festival, Crowley, Louisiana; Mr. George R. Smith, Swiss Festival, Sugarcreek, Ohio; Messrs. Reginald Cunningham, treasurer, David Bryson, publicity chairman, and Robert Wilson, president, the Round Hill Scottish Games Association, Greenwich, Connecticut; Mr. Lyman L. Cantwell, secretary, and Mrs. Judy Klahn, Chamber of Commerce, Stoughton, Wisconsin; Mr. Phil Davis, chief, Community Relations, Texas Tourist Development Bureau, and Ms. Cindy Williams, secretary, Texas State Arts and Crafts Fair, Austin, Texas; Mr. Jarvis Harriman, executive director, Tucson Festival Society, Tucson, Arizona; Mrs. Betty Hatch and Mrs. M. McLaren, Mrs. H. Gilmore and Mrs. D. French of the Fall Festival Committee, West Danville, Vermont.

 *Foods from Harvest Festivals and Folk Fairs*

Introduction

When a Circleville, Ohio, merchant set out a display of pumpkins and corn fodder in front of his shop in the autumn of 1903, he had no way of knowing that his seasonally inspired decorating efforts would be the start of what is now one of America's oldest harvest festivals. Neighboring merchants followed his example, and pumpkins became the theme of local doings that soon included pumpkin-pie bake-offs and vegetable-growing contests. The Pumpkin Show is now an annual event, and while the festival today features band concerts, parades, and other entertainment, pumpkins still remain the number-one attraction. All-time favorite pumpkin pies are baked in competition, auctioned off, used in pie-eating contests, and sold in booths, and other pumpkin treats—soup, milk shakes, cookies, waffles, doughnuts, and even pumpkinburgers—are offered to please the many pumpkin lovers in attendance.

As the pumpkin reigns supreme each October in Circleville, so do raspberries, raisins, rice, and ramps become centers of attention at festivals in other parts of the nation all through the year. Harvests of vegetables, be they onions, carrots, or soybeans, cause people to gather together to celebrate in old-fashioned and new-fashioned ways the wonders and abundance of local crops and to share in their goodness. Fruit festivals pay homage to the apple, cherry, persimmon, orange, or watermelon, and wine festivals give thanks and full credit for being to the grape. Admiration and appreciation of crops and livestock from American farms have brought into being hundreds of county, state, and multistate agricultural fairs all over the land.

But the great numbers of annual American fairs are not restricted to harvest celebrations alone. The bounty of our lakes, rivers, and oceans has inspired an array of piscatorial festivals that range from simple community fish fries, clam, shrimp, and crayfish festivals, lobster feasts, and seafood festivals, where emphasis is all on eating, to trout derbies, fishermen's reunions, and whalers' festivals, where one has the added enjoyment of watching the fishing fleets being blessed, cheering on the whalers in simulated harpooning demonstrations, and seeing or competing with fishermen, both amateur and professional, in trawl-baiting, hauling, sailing, fish-filleting, and many other fishing-related skills.

Some of the most pleasurable festivals from a gastronomic point of view are those held to honor one regionally favorite dish, such as chili con carne in Texas. These affairs praise the attributes of such diverse foods as sauerkraut, kolacky (a kind of pastry), apple butter, bratwurst, or bear meat.

The real purpose of attending one of these events is to quite openly gorge oneself on the specialty of the festival, and, in some cases, to buy even more for later at-home consumption. With sated palate and full stomach, the festival-goer can then go on to watch the high-spirited competition at cook-offs, where qualified contestants vie to turn out the best of home-perfected versions of the fair's specialty. In Gonzales, Louisiana, for instance, competitors carefully tend rice-laden pots of jambalaya, which they cook over hickory-wood fires in the hope of winning the coveted title World Champion Jambalaya Cook for the year.

Exotic ethnic fairs are a food lover's dream come true. There are German, French, Swiss, Italian, Pennsylvania Dutch, and many other fairs organized by various nationalities of people whose forebears settled in America. These people find pleasure in working together to present authentic and well-prepared international food specialties in great variety and abundance. For example, at Danish Days in Solvang, California, a town settled entirely by Danish people, one can feast on Danish aebleskiver (pancakes), renowned Danish open-faced sandwiches, Danish meatballs and red cabbage, and Danish pastries. At the Feast of San Gennaro, New York City's most famous street fair, Neapolitan treats such as calzone (a meat- and cheese-filled turnover) and zeppole (a chewy doughnut) are dispensed by the millions; and at the Kutztown Festival in Pennsylvania, one can literally spend days trying all the Pennsylvania Dutch dishes available and learning about regional cooking, crafts, and farm life.

Gourmets and gourmands alike have food fairs and festivals of all kinds at their disposal in every part of the United States at all seasons of the year. In the West there are American Indian festivals featuring genuine Indian food; in the East, German festivals serving sauerbraten, beer, and black bread; in the North, lumberjack carnivals dishing out woodsmen's food; and in the South, mountain folk festivals with real hill cooking. Date festivals are held in the winter, maple festivals in the spring, potato festivals in the summer, and peanut festivals in the fall.

Beyond the obviously food-oriented fairs, there are often other festivals or gatherings where gastronomic gems and oddities are to be found. One can stumble on a church supper fancily featuring roast goose arranged on platters trimmed with carved oranges and served on tables decorated with bubbling fountains. Driving through the Midwest, one can happen on a festival centered around a parade of biblical floats, and find that the surprise feature of the event is a free, albeit modest, dinner served to anyone attending.

Many of the most provocative of such feasts, fairs, festivals, and happenings from twenty-two states are gathered together in this book and reviewed not only for your armchair enjoyment but for use as a guidebook to any of the events that might tempt you to attend.

At the end of each chapter you will find a paragraph called Festival Facts, which lists the year each festival or fair began, when and where it is held, road directions, where necessary, for reaching it, and whom to contact for any other information you may need.

The recipes of the foods that have made each fair outstanding have been begged, borrowed, and otherwise collected from the cooks, housewives, caterers, competitors, exhibitors, prizewinners, volunteers, and others who participate in the fairs, thoroughly tested for use in the home kitchen, and presented here in authentic form for you to make and savor at will. I hope you'll find these recipes as inspiring and satisfying as I've found the experience of talking, corresponding, and working with festival cooks all over America.

Apples for Everyone

1

"He planted seeds . . . that others might enjoy," and enjoy them they do in abundance at apple festivals from New England to the Ohio Valley every year. The tribute above is to John Chapman, whom most of us know as Johnny Appleseed. His lifetime of apple-tree planting and nurturing led to the establishment of orchards that thrive today through a vast part of the United States and make it possible for many of us to enjoy apples all year long, as well as at festival time, when we honor the beloved fruit and its patron saint of the American orchard.

APPLE FESTIVAL
Colchester, Connecticut

The neat white New England clapboard Congregational Church of Salem in its rural setting seems a perfect place for Colchester's annual Apple Festival. Approaching the lawn of the church, one sees apple-cheeked clowns blowing up apple balloons for the children, and rows of apples hanging from strings to tempt youngsters to try their luck at apple biting in midair. For those with a minimum of patience or luck, the alternative is to take a bite instead from the nice bright candied apples available at the outdoor food booths. For more grown-up tastes, apple fritters at ten cents each are a popular item and attract a line of potential buyers, as do the apple pancakes. Cider is served by the glass and can also be bought by the gallon. Homemade apple jelly and apple butter are for sale, and while making up their minds about such purchases, visitors are serenaded with country music supplied by a banjo–guitar–bass-viol quartet. If the day is fair, lawn chairs are provided for fall sun-worshiping or for those who want to just sit and think about apples.

Inside the church are apple treats galore. There's a tearoom decorated in the applemost manner possible. Tables are covered with apple-printed cloths and hold apple-shaped vases of flowers. Apple-shaped menus list apple pancakes, apple pies, apple betty, and apple muffins made and served by men, women, boys, and girls clad in apple-red blouses, shirts, dresses, vests, or pinafores. For those who need to keep an eye on the time, there's even an apple-shaped clock on the wall.

The work to bring about the apple festivities is done by the members of the church, who spend many weeks baking, sewing, doing handcrafts, and making plans and preparations for their one-day festival. A major cooperative event is the apple-pie baking, for to turn out the more than six hundred pies sold, the women need to work for six weeks, each one doing a particular job, such as peeling apples, slicing them, arranging them in pie shells, and so on, that leads to the finished product. Most of the pies are frozen and sold in a bakeshop set up in the lower part of the church. Here one can also buy apple muffins, applesauce cakes, apple cookies, apple brownies, and other apple baked goods to take home.

Apples appear, too, in forms other than the edible variety. Counters display charming handmade pins and earrings made from apple seeds. Other handmade items include apple-shaped suet feeders for birds, witches with dried-apple heads, wool-embroidered belts and handbags with apple motifs, apple bean-bags, pot holders, and neckties, and paperweights with apple seeds encased in clear plastic.

Not handmade, but nevertheless in the spirit of things, are apple appliqués for sewing onto clothing, apple-printed stationery, Johnny Appleseed jigsaw puzzles, needlepoint kits in apple designs, apple cookbooks, and many other items. One senses these things have been collected with careful thought to avoid any apple-unrelated items.

One of the most popular foods served at the festival is apple pancakes, and the mix for them is also sold at the festival. The following recipes are for Apple Pancakes as made by the Salem Congregational Church people, and for Apple Brownies, one of the popular items sold at their downstairs apple bake sale.

APPLE PANCAKES

> 1^1/$_2$ *cups flour*
> 3^1/$_2$ *teaspoons baking powder*
> ^{3}/$_4$ *teaspoon salt*
> 1 *tablespoon sugar*
> ^{1}/$_2$ *teaspoon cinnamon*
> 1 *egg*
> 1^1/$_2$ *cups milk*
> 3 *tablespoons oil*
> 1 *cup peeled, finely chopped apples*

Sift together into a bowl the flour, baking powder, salt, sugar, and cinnamon. Beat the egg and stir in the milk and oil. Add to the dry ingredients. Fold in the chopped apples.

Pour onto a greased, heated griddle to make pancakes about 5 inches in diameter. Cook until the top is bubbly and the edges begin to brown. Turn and brown the other side. The pancakes will be quite thick. Serve with butter and/or syrup as desired.

MAKES 7 TO 8 FIVE-INCH PANCAKES

APPLE BROWNIES

> ^{1}/$_2$ *cup margarine*
> 1 *cup sugar*
> 1 *egg, beaten*
> 1 *cup sifted flour*
> ^{1}/$_2$ *teaspoon baking powder*
> ^{1}/$_2$ *teaspoon baking soda*
> ^{1}/$_4$ *teaspoon salt*
> 1 *teaspoon cinnamon*
> 1^3/$_4$ *cups peeled, cored, thinly sliced apples*
> ^{1}/$_2$ *cup chopped walnuts*

Preheat the oven at 350°. Cream the margarine until soft, and add the sugar gradually. Add the egg and mix well. Sift together and add the dry ingredients. Fold in the apples and walnuts. The batter will be quite stiff. Spoon into a greased 9-inch-square baking pan and spread out with a rubber spatula. Bake 40 to 50 minutes until a cake tester inserted in the center comes out clean and the brownies pull away from the sides of the pan. Cool on a wire rack in a baking pan. Cut into squares.

MAKES 16

APPLE BUTTER FESTIVAL
Burton, Ohio

Connecticutites not content to stay put arrived in what is now Burton, Ohio, in 1789. They built their New England–style homes around a large village green, so that today a handsome ten-acre park sits in the center of town, surrounded by many stately old homes.

In this setting each fall is held one of Ohio's most homey apple-honoring festivals, the Apple Butter Festival. Giant copper caldrons of apple butter simmer over wood fires, and the tantalizing cooking aroma attracts townspeople and visitors alike to come and sample the pungent treat spread on bread and served piping hot. For at-home eating, the apple butter is packed and sold in pint and quart jars.

A firemen's ox roast and flea market are held on the same weekend as the Apple Butter Festival, and the town's museum and Pioneer Village, where local historical objects are preserved, provide more than enough pleasant activity to fill a day's visit.

For those who can't wait from one year to another to sample some of the more than twelve hundred gallons of apple butter made yearly at the festival, the village Historical Society has provided an official home-size recipe for making their festival Apple Butter.

APPLE BUTTER

> 3 *quarts fresh sweet apple cider*
> 8 *pounds ripe, well-flavored apples*
> 2$^1/_2$ *cups brown sugar, firmly packed*
> 2 *teaspoons cloves*
> 2 *teaspoons cinnamon*
> 1 *teaspoon allspice*
> 1 *teaspoon salt*

Cook the cider over high heat, uncovered, about 30 minutes, or until reduced by half. Meanwhile, wash, peel, core, and quarter the apples. Add to the cider and cook over low heat until very tender. Stir frequently until the apples are of puree consistency. Stir in the brown sugar, cloves, cinnamon, allspice, and salt, and cook over very low heat, stirring almost continuously, until the apple butter thickens. Pour into 1-pint jars and seal securely.

MAKES 1 $^1/_2$ TO 2 QUARTS

JACKSON COUNTY APPLE FESTIVAL
Jackson, Ohio

There's probably room for four thousand and twenty blackbirds to be baked in a pie equal to the size of the ten-feet-in-diameter apple pie baked annually for the Jackson County Apple Festival. Touted as the largest of all the world's apple pies, the mammoth pastry, containing twelve hundred pounds of apple filling clothed in six hundred pounds of dough, is indisputably the ogling center of the festival. The question that pops to mind is where such a monstrous pie could be baked, and the answer is in the ovens of the Goodyear Tire and Rubber Company, presumably when there are no tires baking.

Bigness in apples seems to fascinate Jacksonians, for in addition to the gigantic pie displayed at the festival they have also colored the town's two-hundred-thousand-gallon water-storage tank to look like a giant apple. The "Big Apple," bright red with painted-on green leaves and a sporty brown stem, is a landmark visible for miles in every direction.

But there are standard-sized real apples to see at the festival itself. There's a thirty-two-foot-long and four-foot-high display of Red and Golden Delicious, Rome Beauty, and Jonathan apples in front of the grandstand, and similar displays, both large and small, at various areas of the festival. One isn't confined to just looking at apples, though, but can choose among apple foods aplenty. There are, naturally, fresh, crisp apples, apple cider, and candy apples. There's also tantalizing apple ice cream, and both commercial and homemade varieties are available. The recipe for the scrumptious Apple Ice Cream served by one of the church groups is given below. Apple butter is made and sold, and one can also buy fresh apple pies, apple crisp, and applesauce.

For those who think they can make apple pies better than anyone else in town—a popular opinion, since apple growing is one of Jackson County's leading industries—the Apple Pie Baking Contest is held. Pies, which are baked at home and brought in for judging, can have plain, fancy, or latticed tops, and the judges look not only for tenderness, flakiness, and flavor of the crust, but for tenderness and taste of the apples, consistency and flavor of the filling, and overall looks of the pie. Each entrant has her own surefire method of making an apple pie, and these "secrets" range from using the apples that grow in her own backyard to using a special brand of shortening for the crust or a special touch of spicing.

Other events at the three-day Apple Festival include such diverse entertainment as Little Miss Apple and Apple Festival Queen Contests, karate demonstrations, a champion foxhound show, rock and other bands, water fights between local fire departments, kids' apple-pie-eating contests, and parades.

APPLE ICE CREAM

2 eggs
¹/₂ cup heavy cream
¹/₂ cup sugar
1¹/₂ teaspoons vanilla extract
1 fourteen-ounce can sweetened condensed milk
1¹/₂ cups thick, unsweetened applesauce
1 teaspoon cinnamon
1 tablespoon lemon juice
2¹/₂ cups milk

Combine the eggs, heavy cream, sugar, and vanilla extract in a bowl, and beat well with an electric mixer. Add the condensed milk, and stir well with a spoon. Combine the applesauce, cinnamon, and lemon juice, and add to the first mixture. Add the milk and stir well.

Freeze in an ice-cream freezer according to manufacturers' directions, or pour into a metal pan and place in the freezer. Freeze until slightly firm, about 1 hour. Turn into a bowl, beat well with an electric mixer, and pack into plastic containers. Cover and freeze until firm.

MAKES 2 QUARTS

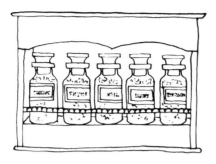

Festival Facts

The Apple Festival, which began in 1971, is held annually on a Saturday in late October at the Congregational Church of Salem, Route 85, Colchester, Connecticut. For further information, write: Apple Festival Committee, % The Congregational Church of Salem, Colchester, Connecticut 06415.

The Apple Butter Festival, which has been held for about thirty-five years, takes place annually on a weekend in early October on the Geauga Historical Grounds in the center of Burton, Ohio, which is at the intersection of Routes 87 and 700. For further information, write: Geauga County Historical Society, Box 153, Burton, Ohio 44021.

The Jackson County Apple Festival, which began in 1937, is held annually for three days, including a weekend, in mid-September in Jackson, on U.S. 35, in southeastern Ohio. For further information, write: Jackson County Apple Festival, P.O. Box 8, Jackson, Ohio 45640.

There is also a Johnny Appleseed Festival held at a time similar to the Jackson County Apple Festival, in Lisbon, Ohio, in the state's leading apple county. For further information, write: Johnny Appleseed Festival, % Chamber of Commerce, Village Hall, Lisbon, Ohio 44432.

National Basque Festival

2

Elko, Nevada

You don't have to pay fifty dollars for a loaf of sheepherders bread at Elko's National Basque Festival, but it's fun to watch when bids run that high in the auction that follows the Sheepherders Bread Contest, one of the many fascinating events that take place at one of the most singular festivals in our country. The high, round, ring-patterned-top loaves of bread which must be evenly formed, light golden-brown in color, and fine and light in texture to win the contest, are, more often than not, baked by men. This seems logical since the bread was originally made by Basque sheepherders in the remote rangelands of the West, where the only available baking pan was a Dutch oven, a heavy black bale-handled covered pot, brought along to double as a stew pot, and the only available oven was one created by digging a pit, building a fire in it, setting in the pot, and baking the bread, covered by earth, until time and instinct dictated its removal.

Time and circumstances have changed the baking style, and today sheepherders bread is baked in a conventional oven, but still in the traditional covered pot. Anyone may enter the Sheepherders Bread Contest, and while each person has his own pet recipe, they are all basically the same. Anita Orbe Mitchell, who's been baking the bread for more than thirty years, won a recent contest, and the prize recipe for her handsome Sheepherders Bread is given below.

When the Basques, one of the world's oldest peoples, who can trace their race back for literally thousands of years, say "Orgi etorri," they're saying "Welcome" to their festival in Euzkera, the ancient Basque language. No matter how heartily this may be spoken, though, it can in no way compare with the Irrintzi Contest, which follows and might be classified as a Basque yelling contest. Originally a war cry, the yell is a long, wavering one that has been described as something between a laugh, a shriek, and a horse's neigh. Today the Basque yell is reserved for lung-stretching exercises only at festivals.

Strenuous weight-maneuvering competitions are vigorously engaged in by very firmly statured, often black-beret-clad Basque males. The extraordinary contests include pulling a 1,500-pound concrete block as far as possible in five minutes, lifting a 250-pound log-shaped weight as many times as can be done in two three-minute periods, carrying a 104-pound, square-shaped, handled weight in each hand over a 100-foot course, and lifting an incredibly large, 225-pound granite ball to the shoulder, circling it about the neck, and repeating the procedure as many times as endurance allows during a three-minute period.

A small, hard ball is hit bare-handed by faster-moving but equally sturdy men in the North American Basque Handball Championship held annually at the festival. Said to be a game originated by the Basques, the handball competition attracts wide attention, with such notables as the consul general of Spain in San Francisco sometimes coming to award the trophies.

Sheep hooking, a contest that originated in Elko, was conceived by area sheepherders who catch the animals and tie them to a post as part of their job during lambing. At the festival, prizes go to those who catch two sheep and tie them up the fastest. Like the bread contest, sheep hooking is one of the offshoots of the original occupation of all the Basque settlers in Elko County. These people, who in the 1870s came from the roughly 50-mile-square Basque provinces situated in Spain and France at the extreme western end of the Pyrenees along the Bay of Biscay to work as sheepherders in Nevada, became the backbone of the open-range sheep industry in that part of the frontier. Needless to say, many of their descendants have forsaken the livestock business for more urban occupations, but interest in sheep-related activities and devotion to Basque tradition is still firm.

The Basque Festival Feed is the food highlight of the two-day event, with garlic-scented barbecued lamb steaks and chops quite rightly leading the way on the menu. In past years Elko men would trek off into the mountains to gather mahogany wood for the barbecue fires, but since the wood is now too rare and difficult to find, it has been replaced by charcoal in the grills. For those who choose to pass up barbecued lamb, there are also beef steaks, and "Chapo" Jose Leniz, chief cook of the festival, who oversees the barbecuing, also sees to the making of Basque beans (or sheepherder beans as they are sometimes called), hearty kettles of pinto beans flavored with chorizos, ham hocks, and bacon. Mr. Leniz has provided his recipe for Basque Beans, which are made up in lots of 250 pounds of beans to 65 pounds of meat cooked for nine hours for the festival. But I've worked out a scaled-down version that can be made at home with just 3 pounds of beans in a third of the time. Green salad and rolls accompany all the meat dishes, and wine and brandy flow generously. Cakes and coffee fill any remaining chinks one may have in the stomach.

All through the festival, snacks are available, with the favorite being chorizos cooked whole in deep oil and served in buns or French rolls in the same manner as hot dogs. Hundreds of pounds of these sausages are made especially for the festival each year, and no accompaniments are served with them to interfere with their special flavoring of sweet (never hot) dried red peppers and mild garlic. Most Basques like to wash down their chorizos with some beer or red wine, but soft drinks can be had, too.

More than five thousand people from all over the United States attend this biggest of all America's Basque festivals annually. The majority of visitors are of Basque origin, but many others come, too, attracted by the good food, unusual competitions, excellent dancers, and frank curiosity. Traditionally, as at most Basque festivals, a Mass is said in the Basque language on Sunday in the town park. Also traditional is the wood-chopping contest, which tests to see who can first chop his way through seven logs, each averaging fifty-five inches in circumference. The contestants, quite frighteningly, stand on top of the logs, which lie on their sides, and aim below their feet with their axes. These tools are imported from Spain especially for the occasion, and there's a first prize of three hundred dollars for the man who can best wield them. During some festival years the National Basque Festival features a sheep dog exhibit for display and comparison of the shepherd's best friend. So dear is the dog to his herder that by camp custom a herder slashes the sign of the cross on top of his loaf of sheepherders bread and tosses the first piece to the dog before proceeding with his own meal.

The prettiest sight of all at the Elko Festival is the joyous Aranak dancers, dressed in white frilled blouses, white off-the-face head wraps, black-laced bodices and aprons, swirling red skirts, and dancing shoes that lace crisscross up to the knees. Performing dances passed down through generations, the girls are particularly picturesque doing the zinta dantza, or ribbon dance. Here they dance around what we would call a maypole, twining the pole with a uniform basket weave of red, white, and green ribbons (the colors of the Basque flag) as they perform their steps, only to reverse their direction and completely unwind the ribbons at the finish. There are jota dance contests for a junior group of girls and boys under twelve, as well as for a regular group. Dancing is also provided by male participants, some invited from Basque communities outside of Elko, many of whom sport red, rather than black, berets in honor of the festival day. After viewing an entire dance program, one has to agree that dancing is indeed the supreme Basque art form.

SHEEPHERDERS BREAD

3 cups hot tap water and boiling water, mixed
²/₃ cup shortening
2 packages active dry yeast
¹/₄ cup sugar
2 teaspoons salt
7 to 8 cups flour

Stir the water and shortening in a bowl until the shortening melts. Cool to lukewarm and sprinkle the yeast over the water. Add the sugar and salt, and stir until the yeast dissolves. Allow to stand in a warm place 5 to 10 minutes, until foamy. Add 4 cups of the flour and beat well with a wooden spoon. Add about 2¹/₂ cups more flour and keep working the dough until it is no longer sticky, adding more of the flour as needed. You will use nearly all of the 8 cups of flour. When the dough is no longer sticky, place on a floured board and knead it until it is satiny. Place it in a greased bowl, cover it, and let it rise in a warm place until doubled in bulk.

Preheat the oven at 375°. Punch down the dough and place it in a greased 4¹/₂- to 5-quart (9¹/₂- to 10-inch diameter) cast-iron or cast-aluminum Dutch oven, and cover with a very well-greased lid. Allow to rise until the dough touches the lid, which will take 10 minutes or longer. Place the covered Dutch oven in the oven for 10 minutes. Remove the lid and allow the bread to continue baking 35 minutes longer. Turn out on a wire rack to cool.

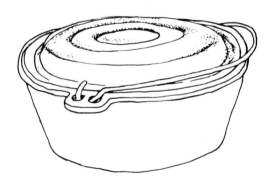

(*Note:* Your loaf will not have a ring-patterned top unless the pan lid has the markings on it.)

BASQUE BEANS
OR
SHEEPHERDER BEANS

3 *pounds dry pinto beans*
1 *or 2 slices bacon, chopped*
1 *medium onion, chopped*
$^1/_2$ *small green pepper, chopped*
1 *ten-ounce can tomatoes*
1 *small ham hock (about* $^1/_2$ *pound)*
1 *two-ounce piece salt pork*
1 *chorizo, cut up*
1 *tablespoon salt (or to taste)*

Pick over the beans carefully, wash them in cold water, and place them in a large bowl. Cover with cold water and soak overnight. The next day, fry the bacon, add the onions and green peppers, and sauté until lightly browned. Add the tomatoes and simmer 15 to 20 minutes. Drain the beans and place in a large pot. Add the tomato mixture, ham hock, salt pork, and chorizo. Add cold water just to cover, and bring to a boil. Reduce the heat and simmer 2 hours, partially covered, stirring occasionally. Add the salt and continue cooking 1 more hour, stirring occasionally.

MAKES 12 SERVINGS

Festival Facts

The National Basque Festival, which began in 1964, is held annually on the first weekend in July in Elko, which is on Interstate 80 in north-central Nevada. For further information, write: National Basque Festival, P.O. Box 1321, Elko, Nevada 89801.

Bavarian Festival

3

Frankenmuth, Michigan

Don your dirndl or your lederhosen and Bavarian hat and come to Frankenmuth, Michigan, to join in a jolly festival that exudes a spirit of fun and conviviality for an entire week each June. Prime up your apppetite and tune up your ear, too, for the food and music are dished out without cessation during this gala Bavarian event.

A quarter of a century ago the festival did not exist. What did exist was a nineteenth-century boardinghouse called the Fisher Hotel, once frequented by lumbermen, but which was steadily declining in patronage and facing the prospect of closing or revamping and expanding. The owners chose the latter course, converted the building to Bavarian styling, and planned a festival for the grand opening of the newly named Bavarian Inn. Favorite German foods were served, and German musicians and entertainers were hired to create a lively and festive atmosphere. The people came, the idea caught on, mushroomed, and quickly outgrew the facilities of a private dining place.

The Bavarian Festival was turned over to the city, which expanded the celebration by putting up large tents in Heritage Park where plump bratwurst, knackwurst, metwurst, sauerkraut, German potato salad, cole slaw (recipe for Bavarian Festival Slaw Dressing follows), barbecued chicken, homemade hot pretzels, stollen, and foaming steins of local beer could be dispensed with room for everyone, and a greater variety and quantity of entertainment could be offered. The whole town took up the theme of the festival and began to construct or convert buildings into Bavarian-type architecture. Businesses were set up to promote the crafts and interests of the townspeople, and soon Frankenmuth became a year-round tourist attraction.

But the Bavarian Festival is what attracts the year's largest crowd. Nearly half a million people visit the town at that time and make awesome inroads on its supply of food and the draft beer that was developed especially for the event. Made by the town's Geyer's Brewery, one of the tiniest in the United States, the Bavarian dark beer became so popular at the festival that it is now sold widely over Michigan throughout the year.

The Bavarian Inn and several other restaurants and biergartens around town also hum with activity, providing entertainment and serving Bavarian foods during the festival. One can choose from among such specialties as sauerbraten with sweetsour gravy, Bavarian potato dumplings, Frankenmuth bean salad, sour cream krautsalat, ente und gans (duck and goose), gefulte kalbsbrust (stuffed veal breast), and wiener schnitzel.

Charlie Kern, whose sausage company makes hearty wursts one can sample at the festival, is proud to point out that there is not a carnival food to be found in the restaurants, in the park, or at any concession stand during the festivities. "What to look for when you travel," he says, "is the kind of food you can't get at home." He's right, but fortunately Frankenmuth was willing to share recipes for some of its German specialties with us, although the only way to get the special wursts is a visit to Frankenmuth.

Food and entertainment go hand in hand at the Bavarian
Festival, and oompah music, singing, and dancing by entertainers as well as dancing by festival visitors to the accompaniment of costumed Bavarian bands goes on daily. There's a
Spas Platz (fun place) for afternoon family entertainment and
evening entertainment and dancing, a water show on the Cass
River, which flows along the park's edge, a Sommer Garten, an
opening-day parade, movies in the Youth Activities Tent, an
Opera Haus which features old-time vaudeville and melodramas
where one is encouraged to hiss the villain and cheer the hero,
and more. There are also more quiet activities on the festival
grounds, such as the Jungviehhof (young animals farm) and the
arts and crafts area.

If you can tear yourself away from the foods, it will be worth
your while to take a stroll or tour around town. One of the local
sights is the glockenspiel tower attached to the Bavarian Inn,
which is something of a local landmark. Imported from
Germany, the thirty-five visible carillon bells in the tower are fit-
ted with a special double keyboard to give the sound of seventy
bells which play merry tunes at three specified hours during the
day. The melodies are followed by an enactment of the story of
the Pied Piper of Hamlin by carved four-and-a-half-foot-high
wooden figures that move on tracks on a stage just below the
bells. The piper, fourteen other figures, and uncountable rats all
move around the stage and disappear through copper doors as the
scenes change and the story progresses.

The Schnitzelbank (woodcarving) Shop is probably the only
one of its kind in this country. Handcarved wooden figurines are
made there by George Keilhofer, who came from Germany to set
up the shop, do his creative work in wood, and act as instructor
to others interested in learning the craft. Some students come
from as far as fifty miles away to attend his classes, and his
figurines are popular items for sale in the shop, along with other
styles of carvings in rare and beautiful woods imported from
various parts of the world.

Another unusual shop (actually three shops) is the
Christmas Shop, which sells Nativity scenes with figures ranging
from half an inch high to life-size, Christmas trees, dolls, elves,
Santa Clauses galore, street decorations, and ornaments by the

dozens. Those who are nostalgic about old-fashioned European Christmas tree ornaments will delight in the sturdy replicas of the rare old fragile originals at modest prices.

Four tours daily are conducted through a large brewing plant in Frankenmuth, and tours of the town, which are offered by jeep, carousel wagon, and bus, can give one a look at what is said to be America's largest family restaurant (Zehnder's), an array of food and craft shops, and a glimpse into the town's past. Frankenmuth, which means "courage of the Franconians," was settled by fifteen Bavarian immigrants who came as missionaries in 1845, and along the tour route one can see a replica of their first building, which is made of rough-hewn cork pine and sits on its original foundation. Alongside it are two mounted church bells which were brought by the settlers from Nuremberg, Germany, and any visitor can feel quite free to ring these Church Bells of the Forest if he feels so inclined. Other sights to see are the historic St. Lorenz Church, which operates one of the largest Lutheran schools in America, the church's museum, and the Frankenmuth Historical Museum, which houses a permanent collection of exhibits from Frankenmuth's past as well as loaned exhibitions from other museums.

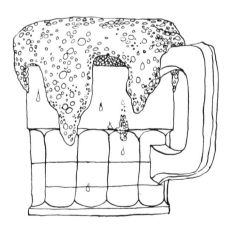

Free shuttle bus service runs between the center of town and the Heritage Park festival area, and to answer questions of all kinds there are information booths manned by knowledgeable Frankenmuthians at strategic locations.

The recipes that follow are for German Pretzels, Bavarian Festival Slaw Dressing, and Sauerbraten with Sweet-Sour Gravy.

GERMAN PRETZELS

FOR THE DOUGH:
   6 *cups milk*
   2 *tablespoons sugar*
   2 *packages active dry yeast*
   6 *tablespoons melted lard*
   2 *tablespoons salt*
   14 *cups flour, more or less*

FOR FINISHING:
   4 *quarts water*
   4 *teaspoons lye*
   Coarse salt (or coarse sea salt)

Heat about ¹/₂ cup of the milk until lukewarm, about 115°. Place in a heated bowl with about 1 teaspoon of the sugar and the yeast, and stir until the yeast is dissolved. Set in a warm place for about 5 minutes until mixture starts to become foamy. Add the balance of the milk and sugar, along with the melted lard, salt, and enough of the flour to make a fairly firm dough. Turn out on a floured board and knead in enough more flour to make a stiff dough. Place in a greased bowl, cover, and set in a warm place to rise for 1 hour. Punch down.

Working with half the dough at a time, and keeping the other half covered, form the pretzels as follows. Pull off a piece of dough about 1¹/₂ inches in diameter, roughly the size of a golf ball. Roll back and forth on a board with the palms of the hands and/or lift up from the board and roll between the hands and pull gently to make a rope about 15 inches long. Note that although the dough will stretch, it will pull back somewhat after it has been made into a rope, so you must end up with a rope at least 15 inches long. Form the rope into an inverted "U" on the board. Pick up the ends and cross them about halfway up. Cross them again, making a double twist. Bring the ends up and over to the curved sides of the pretzel, separating them and pressing each end down against the pretzel. Place on a greased baking sheet, if necessary opening up loops on each side of the pretzel with the ring fingers as you set them down. Allow the pretzels to rise about 30 minutes in a warm place.

Preheat the oven at 400°.

Put 2 quarts of the water in a deep pot (do not use an aluminum or porcelain-coated pot) and bring almost to a boil. Measure 2 teaspoons of the lye* into a long-handled spoon and carefully add to the water. It will sizzle up when added, so stand back from it. Bring to a boil. Place the pretzels, one at a time, in a skimmer and dunk into the boiling solution. Remove and drain on clean, wet dish towels. Sprinkle the pretzels with coarse salt. Place on greased baking sheets. Bake about 15 minutes, until golden-brown. Remove to a wire rack. Can be eaten hot or cold.

Proceed making pretzels with the other half of the dough, punching down the dough before forming the pretzels, and making a fresh solution of 2 quarts water with 2 teaspoons lye.

MAKES ABOUT 6 DOZEN

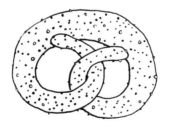

---

*If you are not familiar with working with a lye solution, you may prefer a substitute (although not authentic) of using 2 quarts of water with 8 teaspoons baking soda and 5 teaspoons ammonium carbonate, which may be purchased at drugstores. The sizzling will occur, and the entire balance of the procedure will be the same.

BAVARIAN FESTIVAL SLAW DRESSING

2 *cups salad dressing (not mayonnaise)*
3 *tablespoons white or cider vinegar*
5 *tablespoons sugar*
3 *tablespoons evaporated milk*

Combine ingredients and mix with shredded cabbage as desired to make slaw. Finely chopped onion, shredded carrots, and chopped green pepper or celery may also be added to taste. Cover and chill before serving.

MAKES ABOUT 2½ CUPS DRESSING

SAUERBRATEN WITH SWEET-SOUR GRAVY

1 *four- to five-pound piece bottom round, cross rib, or top sirloin of beef*
Oil or fat for browning

FOR THE MARINADE:
1 *quart water*
1 *cup vinegar*
2 *medium onions, sliced and separated into rings*
1 *cup scraped, sliced carrots*
1 *garlic clove, slightly crushed*
$^1/_2$ *cup sugar*
1 *tablespoon salt*
2 *bay leaves*
4 *or* 5 *peppercorns*
$^1/_4$ *teaspoon thyme*
2 *whole cloves*

FOR THE GRAVY:
1 *teaspoon marjoram*
2 *teaspoons salt*
$^1/_3$ *teaspoon pepper*
1 *bay leaf*

¹/₃ cup tomato paste
3 cups beef stock
¹/₄ cup chopped celery
1 teaspoon chopped parsley
¹/₄ cup red wine
Flour for thickening

Combine the marinade ingredients in a large ceramic, glass, or porcelain bowl or similar container. Add the beef. If there is not sufficient liquid to just cover the meat, add enough water and vinegar in the proportion of 1 part vinegar to 4 parts water to just cover meat. Cover and refrigerate 3 to 4 days, turning meat two or three times a day.

Remove the meat from the marinade, reserving the marinade, and pat the meat dry with paper towels. Brown on all sides in the fat or oil. Add 1¹/₂ cups of the reserved, strained marinade, enough onion taken from the marinade and finely chopped to measure a heaping tablespoon, enough carrot taken from marinade and finely chopped to measure a heaping tablespoon, and all the gravy ingredients except the flour. Bring to a boil, lower the heat, cover, and simmer 2¹/₂ to 3 hours, until very tender. Remove and slice the meat. Thicken the gravy with a few tablespoons of flour mixed with a little cold water. Pour over the sliced meat.

MAKES ABOUT 8 SERVINGS

Festival Facts

The Bavarian Festival, which began in 1959, is held annually during the second full week in June. It is centered at Heritage Park on Weiss Street in Frankenmuth, Michigan. Frankenmuth is east of Route 75 and can be reached by taking Birch Run Exit going north, or Bridgeport Exit going south. For further information, write: Frankenmuth Chamber of Commerce, 635 South Main Street, Frankenmuth, Michigan 48734.

Biblesta

4

Humboldt, Kansas

If you think there's nothing free anywhere under the sun these days, consider heading for Humboldt, Kansas, a little town about halfway between Kansas City and Tulsa, Oklahoma, to attend its Biblesta festival. Each year townspeople from bankers to boy scouts give their time, effort, or money to help plan, build, and present an impressive parade of thirty or more floats depicting stories from the Bible that range from Adam and Eve to the burning bush and Noah's ark. Clubs, schools, civic organizations, and city fathers volunteer to attend to the myriad details that make Biblesta day a success, such as decorating shop windows with miniature biblical scenes or arranging for inspiring speakers and musical groups to appear. Nearly everyone joins in the community effort, not the least of these the ladies from local churches who busy themselves days before the event working out particulars for their singular Free Bean Feed.

In the wee hours of the morning on Biblesta day, these ladies set twenty-eight well-scrubbed iron kettles over twenty-eight well-built open fires, fill them with 1,000 pounds of presoaked beans, 350 pounds of ham, and countless onions, and begin cooking and stirring a meal that will simmer slowly for hours until serving time in the late afternoon. Local people, familiar with the proper procedure for the Free Bean Feed, appear at five o'clock armed with their own table service, and are presented with the lovingly prepared beans and ham served with fresh bread and steaming coffee.

The recipe that follows has been scaled down from 1,000 pounds to a mere 1 pound of beans to make four generous portions that taste almost as good as though they were free.

FREE BEAN FEED

> 1 *pound dry beans, such as Great Northern beans*
> 2 *quarts cold water*
> $^1/_3$ *to* $^1/_2$ *pound smoked picnic ham*
> 1 *generous cup chopped onions*
> 1 *teaspoon salt*

Wash and pick over the beans. Soak overnight in cold water to cover. Drain and rinse.

Place the beans in a large pot with the 2 quarts cold water, smoked picnic ham cut into $^3/_4$-inch cubes, chopped onions, and salt. Bring to a boil, lower the flame, cover partially, and allow to simmer, stirring occasionally, about $2^1/_2$ hours, until beans are soft but not mushy and all liquid is absorbed. Serve immediately with a crisp salad and fresh dark bread if desired.

SERVES 4

Festival Facts

Biblesta, which began in 1958, is held on the first Saturday in October in Humboldt, which is on U.S. 169 in southeastern Kansas. For further information, write: Allen Wilhite, Publicity Chairman, Biblesta, Humboldt, Kansas 66748.

Canada's National Ukrainian Festival

5

Dauphin, Manitoba, Canada

Should your travels take you to the upper portions of Minnesota
or North Dakota, keep the motor running and go on to Dauphin,
150 miles above the North Dakota boundary as the crow flies, to
attend one of the gayest annual events on either side of the
border. While Ukrainian festivals and street fairs do take place in
the United States, none of them reaches the magnitude of
Canada's National Ukrainian Festival, a living monument to the
country's encouragement of unified but separate and individual
cultures. This "mosaic-type" rather than "melting-pot" approach
to the country's multicultural population has helped to preserve

the splendid heritage of Dauphin's original settlers from the Ukraine.

These people came to Manitoba before the turn of the century in answer to a call from the newly formed province for agricultural peoples from other nations to accept free land, build homes, and farm the rich black earth. They packed scythe, sickle, sunflower, poppy, and grain seeds, a handful of native soil, and a good deal of determination, and came to the New World. Because the Canadian prairies so much resembled the Ukrainian steppes, and since the settlers were not unfamiliar with rugged winter weather, they quickly adapted to their new land. The Dauphin area, with its rolling hills, wooded lands, rivers, and streams, was particularly attractive, and here many cleared the land and built wooden homes much in the style they had known in the Old World. Until recent years, a careful eye could spot one of these pioneer thatched-roof houses in the countryside, but now exhibits of scale models such as the ones at the festival must suffice as historical reminders of the originals.

When the Ukrainians came to Canada, they brought with them many fine folk arts and other means of expression such as pysanka (Easter egg decorating), embroidery, woodworking, making and playing of musical instruments, dancing, and cooking. Not the least of these arts was breadmaking, which the people, having lived in the center of a prolific wheat-growing area, had practiced for generations. It is still considered a fine art today, as one can see by looking at the displays of traditional Ukrainian breads in the Fine Arts Center at the festival. There are examples of paska, kolah, babka, zavyvanets, rohalyky, pampushky, korway, and other outstanding examples of the staff of life. Paska is a rich round Easter bread with elaborate dough ornaments, and it is made with special care since it is one of the foods that are blessed before being served at Easter breakfast. Rohalyky are crescents, with or without fillings, their name deriving from the Ukrainian word *rohy,* which means "horns." Korway is a very large bread usually made for wedding celebrations, and it is richly trimmed with dough ornaments and gaily decorated with greenery.

Demonstrations of old-fashioned breadmaking are given during the festival, with simple round loaves of heavenly smelling bread being baked in tunnel-shaped outdoor clay ovens by peasant-costumed ladies and sold to waiting bread lovers.

Nearly as dear as bread to the heart of a Ukrainian is varenyky, more popularly called pyrohy. This pastalike product has as many variations in the dough itself as it does in the fillings. Most often, fillings are made of potato, cottage cheese, meat, fish, mushrooms, sauerkraut, or buckwheat kasha on the one hand, or a number of fruit fillings on the other hand. The festival's foolproof dough recipe with a potato-and-cottage-cheese filling is given below, and foolproof means the varenyky do not come open during cooking, as they are sometimes known to do.

Varenyky-making demonstrations are given in the Fine Arts Center, and not far away on the mall stage, varenyky gluttons take part in the Varenyky Eating Contest. For an entrance fee to cover the cost of the pyrohy to be eaten, and presumably to discourage a mass free-pyrohy feed, one gets to down twenty of the specialties in the briefest time possible, five minutes being the time limit for eating. If you play the game fairly, you take at least one bite from each pyrohy before gulping the balance. Swallowing a pyrohy whole isn't considered cricket any more than slipping one onto your neighbor's plate or under the table. Winners, who have come from as far away as New Jersey, have managed to gobble twenty pyrohy in two and a half minutes or less. Losers often wish they had taken the safe-and-sane approach to pyrohy eating by buying them at one of the festival food stands where they can be properly embellished with salad cream (sour cream), served with fried onions and a sausage or two, and savored in a relaxed manner at a table provided for the purpose.

The various individuals and groups who operate the festival food concessions are as busy dispensing holubtsi (stuffed cabbage rolls) as they are varenyky. Holubtsi is also served with sour cream or plain with baked sausage, and the recipe for sensationally delicious rice-and-mushroom-stuffed holubtsi is given below. Lines form, too, at the festival for bowls of steaming Ukrainian borscht.

Never to be eaten, and sometimes kept for generations, are the beautiful Easter eggs to be seen at Canada's National Ukrainian Festival. Pysanka, the distinct Ukrainian art of egg decorating, is demonstrated at the Fine Arts Center, where numerous exquisite and intricately hand-decorated eggs are on display. Pysanka stems from the verb *pysaty,* which means "to write," and the designs are actually "written" on the eggs with a special stylus heated and dipped in beeswax. The beeswax produces even lines that do not easily smear, and that resist the many dye baths to which the egg is subjected before the wax is melted off to reveal the final design.

An increasingly popular folk art, pysanka has so many practicing craftsmen that a Pysanka Contest is now held at the festival each year with categories open to those of varying degrees of ability. No matter who decorates the egg, though, it always starts off as a smooth, white, uncooked one, and is divided by the artist into sections with basic lines running perpendicularly and/or horizontally around it, with the entire design being based on these divisions. The divisions separate individual motifs, which may be geometric designs or plant or animal symbols, and which can be repeated as few as two or as many as forty times on one egg. Most of the designs are of ancient pagan origin, but each artist's skill and ingenuity is reflected in the arrangement of patterns and motifs and the harmonious use of color. Those who know pysanka can recognize different designs as having originated in different regions of the Ukraine, and may also identify them by variations in coloring. Kits containing dyes, beeswax, patterns, and instructions on how to decorate eggs are sold at the festival.

Decorated eggs are one of the many charming and authentic souvenirs to be found for sale each year. There are also ceramics decorated with traditional Ukrainian designs, hand-embroidered blouses, shirts, and linens, handwoven sashes, embroidery threads, and design books, cookbooks, and stationery with Ukrainian motifs, to name just a few.

One also must not miss the displays of pillows, tablecloths, mats, blouses, and other garments, all beautifully embroidered with designs which originated in different parts of the Ukraine. Some of the embroidery designs have quite possibly been inspired by pysanka designs, and while it's often a matter of debate among Ukrainians which came first, the art of embroidery or the art of egg decorating, it is not disputed that the two arts have influenced one another over the centuries.

Beadwork, usually in the form of necklaces and collars, some lacy in design, others wide and richly worked, is also on exhibit, as well as Ukrainian wood carving in the form of intricately worked and decorated plates, crosses, boxes, vases, and cups. The art of wood carving, or rizba, is also demonstrated, as is the making of Ukrainian musical instruments such as the bandura.

A unique feature at the festival is a special post office set up for the four days during which the event takes place, where letters can be mailed with a special hand-stamped postmark that says "Ukraina," and limited-edition first-day covers are sold.

There's fun to be found at the festival auction, where one can bid on anything from a jar of dill pickles to a piece of pottery, embroidery, or an Easter egg.

Last, or perhaps first, the Ukrainian musicians and dancers at the festival must be seen, and their artistry runs the gamut from the Riding and Dancing Cossacks, who not only perform fast fiery dances but also put their equally spirited horses through grand displays of horsemanship, to the Zirka ("twinkling star") Dance Ensemble, Dauphin's own company of young people of Ukrainian ancestry, whose spirit and spontaneity infectiously capture its audience. Dauphin also boasts a large Festival Choir whose talents have been shared with radio and television audiences as well as with Queen Elizabeth II on one of her visits to Canada. The Canadian National Ukrainian Festival also presents the world's only cymbaly ensemble, the cymbaly, or dulcimer, being one of the world's oldest instruments, and its players few in number. The Ukrainian dulcimer, a prepiano instrument, unlike those in other lands, has 132 to 144 strings and is handcrafted of oak with spruce soundboard and piano-wire strings. The dulcimer ensemble plays strictly by ear, and its repetoire consists of polkas, kozabes, arkans, and the fast-moving kolomayka, music well known to those of Ukrainian heritage.

Concerts on the bandura and the lira are other unusual musical treats to be heard. The bandura, the national folk instrument of the Ukraine, has an oval body and long neck, 50 or so unfretted strings, and a range of three and a half octaves. Its characteristic feature is the treble strings which are struck or plucked with the fingers or fingernails, and its sound is harplike in character. The lira, on the other hand, is a 3-stringed instrument which is hung about the neck on a strap. The player rotates the crank handle hurdy-gurdy—style, and can harmonize with the instrument in song. In years gone by, both the bandura and the lira were played in the Ukraine by singing bards who traveled and sang epic poems and acted as traveling "newspapers" by setting gossip or important events into poetic and musical form.

Musicians, but more especially the dancers, appear in striking costumes. Like other aspects of Ukrainian art and design, costumes vary with the regions from which they come. The headdresses of the girls representing the Poltavian region, for instance, are among the prettiest. Worn off the face, they consist of bright flower wreaths with ribbon streamers attached at either side of the head. A single braid of hair worn down the back bounces and whirls about with the gaily colored ribbons (which signify the number of boyfriends claimed by the wearer) during the lively movements of the dance. Boldly embroidered blouses, shirts, and other garments are worn, and boots and sabers outshine one another, but not the dancers, in some of the cossack numbers.

From the first "Bitaemo" of the hospodar and hospodynia, the host and hostess of the festival, to the last amen at the church service in recognition of the area's Ukrainian pioneers that closes the program on Sunday, one finds endless enjoyment and knows that one is welcome at this queen among festivals.

VARENYKY
(Pyrohy)

FOR THE DOUGH:
> 4 cups flour
> 1/2 teaspoon cream of tartar
> 2 tablespoons oil
> 1 cup (approximately) lukewarm water or skimmed milk

FOR THE FILLING:
> 1/3 cup finely chopped onion
> 1 tablespoon vegetable oil
> 3/4 cup mashed potatoes
> 3/4 cup cottage cheese
> Salt and pepper to taste

FOR SERVING:
> 1/2 cup melted butter
> 1 cup sour cream

FOR THE DOUGH: Combine the flour and cream of tartar. Add the oil and enough water or skimmed milk to make a soft dough. Knead slightly. Cover. Set aside for 30 minutes.

FOR THE FILLING: Sauté the onion in the vegetable oil until soft but not brown. Combine with the mashed potatoes, cottage cheese, salt, and pepper.

TO ASSEMBLE: Roll the dough out thinly, half of it at a time, on a floured board and cut into circles with a round cookie cutter or inverted drinking glass. Working with floured hands, hold a circle in the palm of the hand and place a teaspoon of the filling in the center. Fold in half and pinch and press the edges together to seal securely. Lay on a dry kitchen towel and keep covered while preparing the remaining varenyky.

TO COOK: Drop the varenyky, half a dozen or so at a time, into a large pot of rapidly boiling water. Boil 4 minutes. Lift out into a colander, rinse with hot water, and drain. Coat with melted butter and keep hot until all are cooked and ready to serve.

TO SERVE: Pour the remaining melted butter over the varenyky. Serve with sour cream.

MAKES 3 TO 4 DOZEN

HOLUBTSI

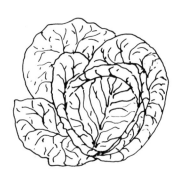

1 *five-pound cabbage*
2 *ounces dried mushrooms*
3 *cups water*
1 *cup chopped onion*
1 *cup vegetable oil*
2 *cups rice*
1 *tablespoon salt*
$^1/_4$ *teaspoon pepper*
2 *cups tomato juice or water*
Sour cream

Remove the core of the cabbage. Submerge the cabbage in a large pot of boiling water and cook, covered, removing the outer leaves as they wilt and draining them in a colander. It will take only a few minutes for each round of leaves to wilt, so make certain not to overcook. When all leaves are removed, line a large casserole with the damaged and very small leaves. With a sharp knife, trim down the back ribs of the remaining leaves so they are fairly thin.

Meanwhile, wash the mushrooms. Simmer them in the water for 1 hour, covered. Strain, reserving the liquid. Chop the mushrooms.

Sauté the onions in $^1/_2$ cup of the vegetable oil.

Parboil the rice 10 to 12 minutes in the mushroom stock, adding enough water to the stock to measure 3 cups. Add the chopped mushrooms, salt and pepper, and half the onions.

To form the Holubtsi, place a tablespoon of filling on a cabbage leaf. Fold the sides toward the center, overlapping them. Starting at the thin outer edge, roll up to the opposite end. Arrange in a casserole in layers as the leaves are filled. Pour in the tomato juice or water. Sprinkle with the remaining $1/2$ cup of vegetable oil and the remaining onion. Cover and bake in a preheated 350° oven for $1^1/2$ hours. Serve with sour cream.

Holubtsi can be reheated in the oven in a casserole, or sautéed in a frying pan.

MAKES 12 OR MORE SERVINGS

Festival Facts

Canada's National Ukrainian Festival, which began in 1966, is held annually for four days including a weekend in late July in Dauphin, which is at the intersection of Routes 20, 5, and 10 in southwestern Manitoba, Canada. For further information, write: Canada's National Ukrainian Festival, 9 Third Avenue, N.W., Dauphin, Manitoba R7N 1H7, Canada.

Carrot Festival and Carrot Recipe Contest

6

Holtville, California

Here's a festival where the cooking contest takes second place to no other event, sharing equal billing with the entire balance of the festival.

People in Holtville, Carrot Capital of the World, "think carrots" all year round. They grow carrots and market them as a business, but think about them just for fun as early as eight months before Carrot Festival time. Then boys and girls tie messages telling about the festival onto balloons and sail them out across the sky from the center of town, each child hoping his or her balloon will travel the farthest and bring a response from the finder. In 1975 Todd Thornburg was one of the children who sent his balloon off into an April sunset from Holt Park, and set the long-distance record that year when his note, sun-scorched and sans balloon, was found by someone out riding in a dune buggy near Yuma, Arizona, the following Christmas Day.

Children join, too, in the Carrot Recipe Contest, and their enthusiasm equals that of the adults. There's a Little Chef's Division for youngsters aged eight to thirteen years, a Junior High Home Economics Division, and a High School Home Economics Division. Winners in these classes are awarded gift certificates as prizes.

Pretty much anyone, anywhere in the world, regardless of age, sex, or place of residence, can join in some category of the Carrot Recipe Contest. The only stipulation is that the recipe entered must contain fresh carrots as an integral part of its makeup. Carrots and/or carrot tops can also be used for garnishing. There are, on an average, eighty entrants each year. Those from other nations submit their recipes by mail, and their dishes are prepared and presented for judging by local cooks, who share the honors with the foreign recipe donor should they win. Visitors are also invited to enter the contest, and, better still, to sample any and all recipes after the final judging. All the carrot recipes are prepared at home and carried into the festival for judging, with the exception of the final Sweepstakes Cook-Off, which is conducted under controlled conditions in the high school home economics kitchen. The recipes are judged on quantity and use of carrots, texture, flavor, presentation, and appearance, and originality or suitability.

While the judges are busy making their decisions, there are other food-oriented programs offered. An example is a demonstration of cheesemaking by a food specialist from the University of California whose easy approach to his subject and amusing chatter during one recent festival kept his audience's interest high. Another demonstration was about microwave cooking, where onlookers could learn some of the tricks of, and advantages to, this newest method of cooking food.

To provide for festival nibbling in the center of activity, the Holtville Chamber of Commerce maintains a large mound of crushed ice where thousands of pounds of crisp, cleaned carrots are available for the taking all during the festival.

The carrot motif is carried out in decorations in the streets, in shop windows, and on parade floats. The ultimate carrot display is at the end of the parade, where there are usually several field trucks loaded with carrots that are distributed along the route of march.

While Holtville enjoys a reputation as the spring training ground for the California Angels baseball team and their farm teams, no human sports competition takes place at the Carrot Festival. However, the animals are kept busy with tractor pulls and a livestock show and exhibition, and the festival parade features many more equestrian participants than floats. A typical Carrot Festival parade also features carrot trucks, local big-name carrot growers riding in antique autos with their families and the Carrot Queen and her Court riding on a Wells Fargo stagecoach.

Other festival attractions include a Fine Arts Exhibit, Arts and Crafts Fair, and Students Art Show. There's a carnival midway for fun and a Carrot Festival Dance at a nearby country club for those who want to dress up to honor the carrot.

The first recipe below is for a taste-laden Carrot Tea Ring baked by John Matlock, the first male Carrot Recipe Sweepstakes winner in two decades. The other prizewinning recipes that follow are for main-dish Carrot Chicken Chinese entered by Mrs. John Poore, Carrot Puffs, which make an unusual dessert, Carrot-Cheese Hors d'Oeuvres to keep in mind for cocktail time, and healthful Holtville Golden Carrot Shake entered by Lucille Leon.

CARROT TEA RING

FOR THE CAKE:
$^1/_4$ cup shortening
1 teaspoon salt
$^1/_2$ cup sugar
2 eggs, beaten
1 cup scalded milk
2 cups grated raw carrots
1 teaspoon grated lemon rind
2 packages active dry yeast
$^1/_4$ cup warm water (about 115°)
5 cups flour

FOR THE FILLING:
2 cups chopped dates
2 cups shredded raw carrots
2 tablespoons lemon juice
Sugar

FOR THE ICING:
1 cup confectioner's sugar, sifted
2 tablespoons warm milk
$^1/_2$ teaspoon vanilla extract
$^1/_4$ cup chopped nuts

In a large bowl, cream the shortening. Add the salt and sugar and mix well. Add the eggs and mix well. Add the scalded milk, carrots, and lemon rind and mix well. Dissolve the yeast in the warm water and allow to stand about 5 minutes, until it begins to foam. Add to the carrot mixture. Add the flour gradually and mix well. Place in a well-greased bowl, cover, and set in a warm place to rise until double in bulk, 1 to $1^1/_2$ hours.

Meanwhile, combine the dates, carrots, and lemon juice for the filling. Punch down the dough, turn it out on a floured board, and knead it until smooth. Take half the dough and roll it out on a floured board in a rectangular shape, $^1/_4$-inch thick. Scatter half of the filling over the dough, sprinkle with sugar, and roll it up like a jelly roll. Form into a ring. Place on a greased baking sheet. With scissors, make diagonal snips about every 2 inches around the outside edge to form a design.

Repeat the rolling out, filling, and shaping with the other half of the dough. Cover and let it rise in a warm place until it doubles in bulk. Meanwhile, preheat the oven at 375°. Bake the rings about 25 minutes. Place on wire racks. For the icing, combine the confectioner's sugar, warm milk, and vanilla extract and drizzle over the tops of the tea rings while still warm. Sprinkle with the nuts.

MAKES 2 RINGS

CARROT CHICKEN CHINESE

2 *large raw chicken breasts, cut in thin strips*
2 *teaspoons soy sauce*
2 *teaspoons fresh ginger, cut in fine dice*
2 *garlic cloves, mashed*
4 *tablespoons sherry*
4 *cups carrots, scraped and sliced very thin*
1 *medium onion, sliced*
1 *medium green pepper, cut in strips*
8 *mushrooms, sliced*
8 *water chestnuts, sliced*
2 *tablespoons soy sauce*
2 *tablespoons cornstarch*
1 *teaspoon monosodium glutamate (optional)*
2 *teaspoons sugar*
Dash of pepper
2 *tablespoons vegetable oil*
2 *tablespoons salt*
1^1/$_2$ *cups drained pineapple cubes*
2 *cups chicken stock*
2 *tablespoons sesame seeds, toasted*

Marinate the chicken strips in the 2 teaspoons of soy sauce, the fresh ginger, garlic, and sherry while preparing the vegetables. Mix together the 2 tablespoons of soy sauce, the cornstarch, monosodium glutamate, sugar, and pepper, and set aside.

Heat the vegetable oil and salt in a frying pan or wok and add the chicken mixture. Stir-fry 3 minutes. Add the vegetables and pineapple cubes and stir-fry 2 minutes longer. Add the chicken stock and cook 3 to 5 minutes longer, stirring occasionally. Add the cornstarch mixture and cook 1 minute, stirring. Garnish with the sesame seeds.

MAKES 6 TO 8 SERVINGS

CARROT PUFFS

FOR THE PUFFS:
   $1/2$ cup boiling water
   $1/4$ cup butter
   $1/4$ teaspoon salt
   $1/2$ cup sifted flour
   1 cup grated carrots
   2 eggs

FOR THE FILLING:
   1 cup milk, scalded
   $1/2$ cup thinly sliced, cooked carrots
   2 tablespoons cornstarch
   $1/4$ teaspoon salt
   $1/3$ cup sugar
   $1/2$ teaspoon vanilla extract

FOR THE PUFFS: Preheat the oven at 425°. Combine the boiling water, butter, and salt in a saucepan and bring to a boil. Add the flour all at once and mix quickly. Remove the saucepan from the heat. Add the carrots and mix well. Add the eggs, one at a time, mixing well after each addition. Drop by tablespoonsful on a greased baking sheet, making 16 puffs. Bake 15 minutes. Reduce the oven temperature to 350° and bake 25 minutes longer. Cool on a wire rack.

FOR THE FILLING: Place the scalded milk in a blender with the cooked carrots and blend until the carrots are thoroughly pureed. In the top of a double boiler, combine the cornstarch, salt, and sugar. Add the milk-and-carrot mixture. Place over hot water and cook, stirring constantly, until the mixture becomes very thick. Remove from heat. Stir in the vanilla extract. Cool slightly.

Punch a hole in the side of each puff and fill with filling forced through a pastry bag.

MAKES 16 PUFFS

CARROT-CHEESE HORS D'OEUVRES

1 *three-ounce package cream cheese*
¹/₃ cup grated raw carrots
1 *tablespoon chopped chives*
4 *drops Worcestershire sauce*
Grated carrots (optional)
Parsley sprigs (optional)

Soften the cream cheese. Add the carrots, chives, and Worcestershire sauce and mix well. Chill and use as a spread for crackers, or chill until firm enough to handle and shape into 10 miniature carrots, covering them with additional grated carrot and inserting tiny sprigs of parsley into the end of each carrot shape to resemble carrot tops.

MAKES ABOUT 1 CUP OF SPREAD,
OR 10 MINIATURE CARROTS

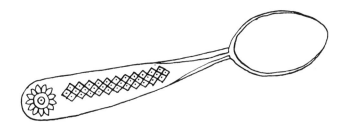

HOLTVILLE GOLDEN CARROT SHAKE

¹/₄ cup orange juice
1 tablespoon grated orange rind
1 tablespoon crushed pineapple
3 tablespoons grated raw carrot
1 pint vanilla ice cream

Place all ingredients in a blender or food processor in the order listed, and blend until creamy. Pour into 1 or 2 glasses. For a thicker shake, more ice cream may be used.

MAKES 1 OR 2 SERVINGS

Festival Facts

The Holtville Carrot Festival and Carrot Recipe Contest, which began in 1948, is held annually during the last week of January or the first week of February for a period of eight or nine days in Holtville, which is on Route 115, four miles north off Interstate 8, in southern California near the Mexican border. For further information, write: Carrot Festival, Holtville Chamber of Commerce, Fifth and Holt, P.O. Box 185, Holtville, California 92250.

National Cherry Festival

7

Traverse City, Michigan

You may have been to a Swedish smorgasbord or a Danish, Norwegian, or Finnish smorgasbord, but you've probably never been to a cherry smorgasbord unless you've visited the National Cherry Festival in Traverse City. The feature of their big Cherry Smorgasbord Luncheon, which includes hearty midday main dishes, is their famed cherry dessert sampling table. Wives of the many local cherry growers whip up all sorts of luscious cherry desserts, arrange them temptingly before you, and invite you to try one, or two, or as many as you like to satisfy your craving for cherry creations. Recipes for two especially delicious desserts from a recent festival, Cherry Meringue Bars and Cherry Jam-Filled Cookies, are included below, and some of the other treats one might try at the smorgasboard include hot cherry cake, cherry pies, cherry cheesecakes, cherry berries on a cloud (meringue), and chocolate cherry bars.

It's easy to understand why the ladies of Traverse City have become so adept at cooking with cherries, since 70 percent of the world's red tart cherries are grown in the state of Michigan, with the greatest concentration of orchards on the Old Mission Peninsula adjacent to Traverse City.

The first National Cherry Festival was created fifty years ago to celebrate the fruit's abundance. Cherry growing had successfully replaced the recently defunct local lumber business, so there was good cause for rejoicing. The festival was held at harvest time, when the orchards were swarming with cherry pickers, summer residents had arrived to join in the festivities, the cherry-processing plants were finishing up the preparation of sweet cherries and getting ready for the inundation of tart cherries, and orchardists' wives were putting up their own fruit, both in the form of fresh cherry treats and canned cherries for winter use.

Joy in the abundance of cherries continues today, and cherry-cooking enthusiasm is shared equally by the adults and the young people of Traverse City, with competition running high at the annual Junior Cherry Recipe Contest held during the festival. Any boy or girl between the ages of eight and sixteen may enter, but must bring along not just one but two batches of his or her favorite cherry recipe to the contest—one for tasting by the judges, and the other for the audience to enjoy. The recipe for good-tasting Cherry Pecan Torte, a recent prizewinner by fourteen-year-old Sue Hammond, is given below.

For children who'd rather eat cherries than cook them, there's a Cherry Pie Eating Contest divided into advancing stomach-capacity groups of ages five to seven, eight to ten, eleven to twelve, and thirteen to fourteen, and anyone attending the festival in these age groups can sign up for the gorging.

To see what's new in cherry cooking, young and old alike gather round at the Cherry Bakefest, where demonstrations are given by local men and women who are dedicated to the making and writing down of cherry recipes and enjoy passing on information about their favorite fruit.

For early risers, the festival features either a Cherry Fritter Breakfast or a Cherry Pancake Breakfast; and for parade followers, there's a cherry ice cream social immediately after the Heritage Parade (one of the three parades held during the week) in the evening. Here, at the Supercolossal Ice Cream Social, one can top off a day of cherry eating with a big cherry sundae, ice cream for which is donated by a national ice cream company that has a retail store in Traverse City. Tickets must be purchased to attend the social, since the funds are used to perpetuate the festival itself.

The organizers of the National Cherry Festival haven't forgotten anyone, and to please the tiny tots, they have a Little People's Cherry Hunt in the park. Armed with paper bags, the children search the grounds to retrieve all the hidden cherries (which, for practicality's sake, are made of plastic) they can find. Each child who participates receives a prize, with a special prize going to the boy or girl who has found the most cherries.

Endless diversion is offered in various locations around town, with many of them at water's-edge parks, at marinas, and along Front Street, which is converted into Cherry Lane for the weeklong festival. Cherry Lane is where a variety of little shops and booths offer cherry desserts, cherry ice creams, and other goodies, where slides and films about the cherry industry are shown, where one can take photos of the National Cherry Queen and her Court, where an information booth is set up, and where one can sign up for one of the cherry orchard tours arranged to let the visitor see the tart fruits growing or being harvested at one of the local orchards. An orchardist usually escorts the group through his grounds, explaining various procedures, giving a shaker demonstration, and in cases where he does his own cherry processing, taking them through his plant. Sometimes cherries or cherry products are offered for sale at farm markets located at the orchards.

While the number of other events that take place at the festival are too numerous to list and vary slightly from year to year, one can count on seeing and/or joining in scads of enjoyable happenings. Some of them might be old-fashioned games in the park, sing-alongs, frog and turtle races, milk carton boat races, twelve-mile bike races, Green Beret mass parachute drops, Mr.

Northern Michigan physique contests, shallow-water tugs-of-war and slippery watermelon recoveries on the beach, children's pet shows featuring the Speediest Rabbit possibly trying to escape from the Best-Dressed Cat, concerts, plays, and model airplane demonstrations—something for everyone.

CHERRY MERINGUE BARS

FOR THE BASE:
$^1/_2$ *cup butter or margarine*
$^1/_2$ *cup confectioner's sugar*
1 *cup sifted flour*
2 *egg yolks*

FOR THE FILLING:
$^2/_3$ *cup sugar*
$2^1/_2$ *tablespoons cornstarch*
1 *tablespoon lemon juice*
1 *sixteen-ounce can tart red pitted cherries packed in water*

FOR THE MERINGUE:
2 *egg whites*
$^1/_2$ *cup sugar*
3 *or* 4 *tablespoons slivered almonds*

FOR THE BASE: Preheat the oven at 350°. Cream the butter or margarine. Add the confectioner's sugar and beat well. Blend in the flour and egg yolks. Spread evenly on the bottom of a greased 9x13-inch baking pan. Bake 15 to 18 minutes until browned around the edges. Set aside on a wire rack.

FOR THE FILLING: Combine the sugar and cornstarch in a saucepan. Stir in the lemon juice and $3/4$ cup of the liquid drained from the can of cherries—if necessary, adding enough water to make $3/4$ cup. Heat, stirring constantly, until the mixture becomes clear and thick. Stir in the drained cherries from the can. Remove from heat. Cool. Spread evenly over the baked base.

FOR THE MERINGUE: Preheat the oven at 350°. Beat the egg whites until soft peaks form. Add the sugar gradually and continue beating until stiff. Spread evenly over the cherry filling. Sprinkle with the slivered almonds. Bake 15 to 20 minutes, until lightly browned. Cool. Cut into bars.

MAKES 16 BARS

CHERRY JAM-FILLED COOKIES

$1/2$ cup butter or margarine
$1/2$ cup shortening
2 cups brown sugar
2 eggs
$1/2$ cup milk
1 teaspoon vanilla extract
$3^1/2$ cups flour
$1/2$ teaspoon salt
1 teaspoon baking soda
$1/2$ teaspoon cinnamon
$3/4$ cup cherry preserves

Cream the butter or margarine and shortening together. Add the brown sugar and mix well. Add the eggs. Add the milk and vanilla extract. Sift together the flour, salt, baking soda, and cinnamon, and add to the butter mixture.

Preheat the oven at 350°. Drop the dough by heaping teaspoonful onto an ungreased baking sheet. With a small spoon make a dent in the center of each cookie. Fill with the cherry preserves. Put a dab of dough on top of the preserves and with the fingers seal in all around so that no preserves show. Bake 11 to 12 minutes, or until lightly browned.

MAKES ABOUT 6 DOZEN

CHERRY PECAN TORTE

FOR THE TORTE:

1 egg

1¹/₄ cups sugar

1¹/₂ cups canned tart red pitted cherries, drained (reserving the liquid)

1 cup flour

¹/₄ teaspoon salt

¹/₂ teaspoon baking soda

1 teaspoon cinnamon

1 tablespoon melted butter

1 teaspoon almond extract

¹/₂ cup chopped pecans

FOR THE SAUCE:

1 tablespoon cornstarch

¹/₈ teaspoon salt

1 cup cherry juice (drained from canned cherries, and water added to make 1 cup liquid)

2 tablespoons sugar

1 tablespoon butter

2 drops almond extract

Whipped cream

FOR THE TORTE: Preheat the oven at 350°. Beat the egg. Add the sugar gradually and beat well. Fold in the cherries. Sift together the flour, salt, baking soda, and cinnamon, and fold into the cherry mixture. Add the melted butter and almond extract. Turn onto a greased, 9-inch-square baking pan and spread out evenly with a rubber spatula. Sprinkle the nuts on top. Bake 40 to 45 minutes. Cool on a wire rack.

FOR THE SAUCE: Combine the cornstarch and salt. Mix with a little of the cherry juice. Add to the balance of the cherry juice and heat in a saucepan with the sugar until clear and thickened. Remove from the heat and stir in butter and almond extract. Cool and cover until serving time. To serve, cut the torte in squares, top with the whipped cream, and spoon the sauce over all.

MAKES 9 OR 16 SERVINGS

Festival Facts

The National Cherry Festival, which began in 1926, is held annually for one week in early July at Traverse City, which is on Route 37, south of Route 72, near the West Arm of Great Traverse Bay, in northwest Michigan. For further information, write: National Cherry Festival, P.O. Box 141, Traverse City, Michigan 49684.

Chili Cook-Off

8

Terlingua, Texas

Every year in early November the remote ghost town of Terlingua, Texas, becomes filled and then overflowing with thousands of people who arrive by car, van, camper, pickup truck,
motorcycle, foot, thumb, horse, and private plane to set up an
overnight community in preparation for a one-day showdown
dear to the hearts of Texans.

The cause of the celebration is the cooking of chili con
carne, if indeed chili can be thought of as a cause. It can to a
Texan, to whom it's as sacred as oil wells, the Alamo, and the
lone star on his state flag. Texans don't make passable chili, good
chili, or even great chili. Each one makes "the best chili in the
world," and the enthusiasm they share in trying to prove it has

given rise to chili cook-offs in cities, villages, and unpeopled places all over Texas. No Texan is content until he's won a chili-making title, and then his only aim seems to be to defend that title the following year and perhaps gain another.

Texans will tell you, tongue-in-cheek, that chili has been made for over three thousand years in their part of the nation, and will produce archaeological chili artifacts of dubious origin to prove it. But the first chili cook-off known to modern man took place in 1967 in uninhabited Terlingua, where the International Chili Society started and continued to hold its annual cook-off until 1975, when it moved to Rosamond, California. But Terlingua goes on holding its own cook-off each year on the sacred ground.

Terlingua, in the midst of southwestern Texas's beautiful mountain-desert landscape, is eight miles from the entrance to Big Bend National Park, which covers a thousand square miles along the Rio Grande, and eighty miles from the nearest town, Alpine. The actual cook-off takes place on the porches of Terlingua's general store and opera house, sites not hard to find, since the only other buildings in town are a schoolhouse, church, post office, and jail.

Once a thriving mercury-mining town, Terlingua was built and owned by a Chicago-based businessman by the name of Howard Perry. Mr. Perry's mansion, which was built for his use during his visits to Terlingua, now lies in ruins, as do the many adobe huts dotted across the hills in which his Mexican mine workers lived. Silence now reigns through most of the year in the ghost town, but the stillness is interrupted when the chili lovers converge for their annual bash.

The cook-off organizers spend no money to promote, talk up, or advertise the cook-off. It just happens, and chiliheads from all over Texas as well as "foreigners" from out of state show up at the right time along with locals, big names, little names, marching bands, television cameramen, beer and water sellers, and anyone else who feels like joining the crowd of eight to ten thousand who come to cook chili, eat chili, hold their breath at chili judging, quaff a glass or two of local beer, kibitz, and enjoy the spirit of conviviality that seems to prevail among chili lovers everywhere.

The only noncordial note ever to come from Terlingua's cook-offs is now, happily, only a memory. To be eligible for the cook-off, a contestant must have won a championship or been runner-up in a previous contest, either at Terlingua or elsewhere. This presented a problem to lady chili-cookers who found themselves barred from entering cook-offs just about everywhere, simply because they were women.

A Houston chili lover named Allegani Jani Schofield was refused entrance to a contest at the Texas State Chili Cook-Off in San Marcos, and set out to put things to rights in the chili-contest world. She and some other ladies of similar persuasion organized a group called the Hell Hath No Fury Susan B. Anthony Memorial Women's Chili Cooking Group. They found a compassionate man who turned his town over to them for their first all-woman chili cook-off. Luckenbach, Texas, was put on the map, and a new era began in chili land.

Texas men, having seen the wisdom of opening chili cook-offs to both sexes, welcomed Allegani Jani to Terlingua's 1971 cook-off, and although she didn't win, she was on her way. Texas writer Sam Huddleston said of her, "My favorite contestant was Allegani Jani Schofield from Houston. Allegani Jani wore a set of hot pants which moved planned parenthood back ten years. This little mistress of the chili pod didn't need to fire off any rockets to get attention. She had it, Gentlemen . . . All of it! One spoonful of Allegani's chili would get an hombre spastic with happiness. I'm glued to the contention that those judges who voted against her surely must have had cases of arrested masculine development."

The rest is history. Jani, in late 1974, won second place in the Carrie A. Nation Memorial Cook-Off, which made her eligible to enter the Terlingua Cook-Off at the end of the year. She won hands down to become the first woman ever to be World Champion Chili Maker. "The hand that rocks the cradle will rule the chili world," said Jani as she stood beside her throat-searing pot of Hot Pants Chili to receive her reward. Her recipes for both Hot Pants Chili and Hot Pants Beans are given below.

The second chili recipe below, Wood's Undenia-Bull World Championship Chili, is that of Mr. C. V. Wood, Jr., who is not only on the board of governors of the International Chili Society, but now acts as the chief tasting judge at its World Champion Cook-Off since he retired as undefeated World Champion Chili Cook. After winning the title for two years, Mr. Wood bowed out to give other chili cooks a chance.

The last recipe below is Ed ("Chill Lee") Paetzel's recipe for World's Greatest Jackrabbit Chili Champion Chili. "Chill Lee" vows that children and people who claim not to like chili are won over by his dish, which he describes as more of a gourmet chili than most. It won him the state Chili Champion title over 144 cooks, and also secured winning place for his daughter, Kim, in the Texas State Junior Championship over 41 cooks.

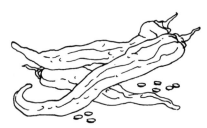

HOT PANTS CHILI

4 pounds stew meat, ground once
3 onions, chopped
2 tablespoons oil
Salt to taste
Pepper to taste
2 heaping teaspoons cumin seeds
6 garlic cloves, smashed
1 or 2 teaspoons water
1 large can tomatoes
1 teaspoon sugar
$^1/_2$ can beer (preferably Pearl Beer)
3 tablespoons chili powder (or, preferably, 1 small pack Vanco chili powder)
2 two-and-one-half-ounce packs Vanco chili seasoning
OR:
  1 teaspoon red pepper flakes
  2 tablespoons ground coriander
  2 tablespoons ground cumin
  4 tablespoons paprika
  2 teaspoons salt

4 teaspoons oregano
2 tablespoons dried onion flakes
1 teaspoon dried garlic flakes
¹/₄ cup cornstarch
¹/₂ teaspoon ground black pepper
3 teaspoons mole paste*
1 teaspoon Tabasco sauce
1 teaspoon salt
1 quart water
4 jalapeño peppers, chopped (remove seeds before chopping if you don't want extremely hot chili)
¹/₂ cup masa flour*
Water

Brown the meat with the onions in the oil. Add the salt and pepper. With a molcajete,† or mortar and pestle, mash and grind together the cumin seeds, garlic cloves, and 1 or 2 teaspoons water. Add to the meat mixture.

In a blender place the tomatoes, sugar, beer, and chili powder. Add the Vanco chili seasoning or the alternate ingredients and blend until the tomatoes are broken up completely. Add to the meat mixture.

Add the mole paste, Tabasco sauce, salt, 1 quart water, and jalapeño peppers. Simmer for 2¹/₂ hours, stirring well from time to time.

Combine the masa flour with enough water to make a runny paste. Add to the chili while stirring quickly in order to prevent lumping. Cook 30 minutes more for the chili to thicken.

MAKES 8 OR MORE SERVINGS

---

*Mole paste and masa flour are available at Mexican and Spanish groceries, specialty food stores, and by mail from such sources as: Frank Pizzini, 202 Produce Row, San Antonio, Texas 78207; Casa Moneo, 210 West Fourteenth Street, New York, New York 10014; and Valley Distributing Co., 2819 Second Street N.W., Albuquerque, New Mexico 87107. Ordinary flour can be substituted for masa flour, although the results will be less authentic.
†A molcajete is a Mexican mortar-and-pestle-type grinder made of volcanic rock.

HOT PANTS BEANS
(To Go with Hot Pants Chili)

Allegani Jani says, "In Texas we don't put beans in our chili, but they're great as a side dish. All you foreigners go ahead and dump them in if you must, but cook them this way *first.*"

1 *pound dried pinto beans*
Cold water
2 *medium-sized onions, chopped*
6 *thick slices bacon, chopped*
1 *tablespoon salt*
1 *can tomatoes (or tomato chilies if you like them hot) (both optional)*
1 *teaspoon sugar (optional)*

Wash and pick over the beans. Place them in a bowl and cover with cold water several inches above the beans. Allow to soak overnight. Drain and place the beans in a large pot with the same amount of cold water as before. Add the onions, bacon, and salt. Add the optional tomatoes and sugar if desired. Allow to simmer 2 hours, watching to see that the water does not boil away completely. If necessary, add a little boiling water from time to time. If too much water remains at the end of boiling, boil down quickly to remove the excess. Taste the beans after 1 hour of cooking and add more salt if necessary.

MAKES ABOUT 6 SERVINGS

WOOD'S UNDENIA-BULL
WORLD CHAMPIONSHIP CHILI

7 cups peeled, chopped ripe tomatoes
$^1/_4$ cup finely chopped celery
2 teaspoons sugar
$^1/_4$ to $^1/_2$ pound beef kidney suet
5 pounds center-cut pork roast or pork chops
4 pounds beef flank steak
8 ounces light beer
1 tablespoon ground oregano
1 tablespoon ground cumin
$^1/_2$ teaspoon monosodium glutamate (optional)
1 tablespoon fine black pepper
4 teaspoons salt
5 tablespoons chili powder (preferably unblended)
1 teaspoon cilantro (coriander leaf or Chinese parsley)
1 teaspoon thyme
5 cups freshly made or canned chicken broth
6 green chilies (Anaheim Green or New Mexican No. 6; or 2 four-
  ounce cans whole or diced green chilies)
2 garlic cloves, finely minced
2 cups Spanish onions, cut into $^1/_4$-inch dice
2 cups green bell peppers, cut into $^3/_8$-inch dice
1 pound Monterey Jack cheese
Juice of 1 lime

Combine the tomatoes, celery, and sugar in a saucepan and simmer about $1^1/_2$ hours, covered, stirring occasionally.

Meanwhile, thinly slice the beef kidney suet and render it in a skillet until most of the fat has melted. Discard the unmelted pieces. Bone out the pork roast or pork chops and cut off any fat. Cut into $^1/_4$-inch cubes. Remove any fat from the flank steak and cut into $^3/_8$-inch cubes.

In a bowl combine the beer, oregano, cumin, monosodium glutamate, black pepper, salt, chili powder, cilantro, and thyme. Put the chicken broth in a large (about 2-gallon) cooking pot. Add the tomato sauce when it has finished cooking. Remove the seeds from the canned chilies and cut into $^1/_4$-inch dice, or prepare the Anaheim Green or New Mexico No. 6 chilies by holding them over an open fire until the skins are seared. Remove the skins and boil the chilies approximately 15 minutes until tender. Remove the seeds and cut into $1/4$-inch dice. Add to the chicken broth mixture, along with the garlic. Add the beer and spice mixture. Bring to a slow simmer.

Meanwhile, sauté the pork cubes in small portions in a skillet in the rendered suet until the pork becomes white on all sides. Do not brown. Add the sautéed pork to the cooking pot, bring to a low boil, and cook about 30 minutes.

Meanwhile, sauté the cubed flank steak in a skillet in the rendered beef suet, a small amount at a time, until the beef has lost its color. Do not allow it to brown. Add to the cooking pot when the pork has cooked for 30 minutes. Cook at low boil about 1 hour.

Add the diced Spanish onions and bell peppers and cook at a low boil 2 to 3 hours, stirring every 15 or 20 minutes. The meat should be very tender but not broken down too much. Remove from the heat. Cool for about 1 hour. Refrigerate for 24 hours.

Reheat the chili or package and freeze it. When reheating, bring it to a slow simmer and heat well. Five minutes before serving time, grate the cheese and add it to the chili. Stir until it has dissolved. Add the lime juice, mix well, and serve with small round soup crackers.

MAKES ABOUT 5 QUARTS

NOTE: Use a wooden spoon, not a metal one, throughout the recipe when stirring the chili.

ED CHILL LEE'S WORLD'S GREATEST JACKRABBIT CHILI CHAMPION CHILI

> 2 pounds ground beef
> 2 tablespoons sugar
> 3 tablespoons dry onion flakes
> 2 tablespoons chili peppers (or dry New Mexican chilies, or a good mild chili powder)

3 tablespoons cumin
1 teaspoon salt
$^1/_2$ teaspoon oregano
1 teaspoon coriander
1 tablespoon thyme
$^1/_2$ teaspoon black pepper
1 tablespoon paprika
1 garlic clove
2 tablespoons masa harina
2 eight-ounce cans tomato sauce, plus equal quantity of water

Brown the beef and drain off any fat. Add all other ingredients and mix well. Cook over low heat 1 hour, stirring occasionally.

MAKES ABOUT 6 SERVINGS

Festival Facts

The Terlingua Chili Cook-Off, which began in 1967, is held for one day early in November in Terlingua, which is on Route 170 west of Route 118, eight miles from Big Bend National Park and near the Mexican border, in southwest Texas. For further information, write: Frank X. Tolbert, The Dallas Morning News Communications Center, Dallas, Texas 75201.

The International Chili Society World's Championship Cook-Off, currently in its eleventh year, is held for one day in late October at Tropico Gold Mine, Rosamond, California, which can be reached from Los Angeles by taking the Golden State, Hollywood, or San Diego Freeway north to the Antelope Valley Freeway (California Highway 14), continuing north to the Rosamond–Willow Springs exit, west three and a half miles to the Tropico Gold Mine sign, and then right for a half mile. For further information, write: The International Chili Society, 8899 Beverly Boulevard, Los Angeles, California 90048.

Christmas at Williamsburg

9

Colonial Williamsburg, Williamsburg, Virginia

> *Now Christmas comes, 'tis fit that we*
> *Should feast and sing, and merry be*
> *Keep open House, let Fiddlers play*
> *A Fig for Cold, sing Care away*
> *And may they who thereat repine*
> *On brown Bread and on small Beer dine*
> *—Virginia Almanack, 1766*

Worth going out of your way to visit at any time of the year, Williamsburg seems especially inviting at Christmastime, when the atmosphere is gay and festive, ceremonies reflect the holiday spirit, and foods take on special interest.

In this happy season, candles shine in windows, wreaths and evergreen garlands decorate doorways, balconies, and the wrought-iron gate of the Governor's Palace. Hardly a mantelpiece is left without an adornment of pine, bayberry, rosemary, ivy, or cherry laurel, or an artful arrangement of apples and holly around pewter plates. Della Robbia wreaths trimmed with oranges, limes, lemons, pineapples, and pomegranates—all known to the Williamsburg people two hundred years ago—add to the beauty of the decorations, as do simple bouquets of holly and other greens.

The Grand Illumination of the City is the official celebration that opens the holiday season about a week before Christmas. Activities abound. There is an Annual Christmas Homes Tour, when private residences are open to the public, a special Christmas Exhibition is shown at the Abby Aldrich Rockefeller Folk Art Collection, there are Greens and Garlands Tours, Christmas Fifing, Beating of the Holiday Drums, Colonial Games, a Community Christmas Tree, a Mummer's Play—in all, about sixty Christmas happenings scheduled for the holiday season.

One of the most popular events of the fortnight celebration is Bringing in the Yule Log, a practice which, surprisingly, dates back to ancient Persia. Then a tree was felled once a year, and a round section cut from its trunk to turn like a wheel. This was marked into four segments, each representing a season of the year. This calendarlike wheel was called a Yole, and the log from which it was cut, a Yole Log. At the beginning of each season, the wheel was turned and a great fire kindled to which the Yole Log was added while the people prayed for their god to be kind to them during the coming season. Later the Britons adapted the custom to their Christian religion, and the name Yole became Yule.

Now each Christmas a Yule Log is hidden somewhere in the woods behind the Williamsburg Inn, and everyone is invited to join in the hunt for it. The finder, or "winner," gets to ride the log, decorated with greens and bright red ribbon, on a wooden skid, and the losers get to pull the rope that drags the skid back to the inn. There the log is carried into the hall on Christmas Eve by costumed waiters, and is cut in two, the idea being to burn one section and to keep the other for kindling the Yule fire the following year.

Before the fire is lit, each guest is provided with a holly sprig with which to touch the Yule Log as it goes by. The holly symbolizes the woes of the past year, and touching the log with it represents the banishment of these woes. After the fire has been lit, all the holly sprigs are tossed in to assure good luck in the future. Wine is poured into the fire during a traditional blessing of the log, and everyone joins in spirited, old-fashioned carol singing. Song-parched throats are eased immediately with servings from the traditional Wassail Bowl, a spiced ale or cider drink. Wassail, from the ancient Saxon words *wass hael,* means "To your health," and the reply to this toast in olden times was "Drink hail," which still seems fitting.

Wassail recipes have changed through the years and have undoubtedly had many variations from family to family. The modern Williamsburg version replaces ale or cider with wine, and the recipe for it is given below, along with one for Williamsburg Holiday Cookies, which are served along with the drink.

A variety of menus is offered at the various Williamsburg hotels and restaurants during the holiday season: the New Year's Eve Dinner, which includes everything from Deviled Cherrystone Clams to French Flutes; the International Christmas Dinner, which includes specialties from ten nations; an Old Dominion Dinner; a Baron's Feast; an Old English Dinner; a Country Buffet and Square Dance; Champagne Breakfasts; a Christmastide Assembly; a Groaning Board; and New Year's Eve parties. The complete Groaning Board menu consists of Virginia Peanut Soup,* Fillet of Fresh Water Trout, Williamsburg Spoon Bread,* Roast Prime Ribs of Beef, Mixed Garden Vegetables, Yorkshire Pudding, Salad of Fresh Garden Greens with French Dressing, Tipsy Squire,* Beverage, Sally Lunn Bread,* and carafes of Red Burgundy. Recipes for all starred items are found below, so that you can recreate a complete Groaning Board in your own home.

In old-time Williamsburg the Christmas holidays were celebrated in particular with church services, feasting, drinking, and dancing at house parties and family gatherings, hunting, "barring out" of schoolmasters to assure stoppage of lessons, and the firing of guns on Christmas Eve, New Year's Eve, and New Year's Day, a custom still reflected in the popping of firecrackers in some areas. It was not a practice to exchange gifts, but slaves were excused from most duties and were given new clothing and shoes and small amounts of money for their "Christmas Boxes." The Christmas tree did not come to Williamsburg until much later, in 1842, when a political exile from Germany introduced the idea to a family whose guest he was for the holidays. They were enchanted with the notion and improvised ornaments from twists of colored paper, hung fruit on the tree, and placed a gilded paper star on top.

Christmas dinner in Williamsburg and other parts of colonial Virginia typically included roast beef, Virginia ham, venison, wild fowl, plum puddings, cakes, and mince pies. No one really knows whether the Yule Log or Wassail Bowl were included in early Williamsburg festivities, for these things go unrecorded. But we do know that huge log fires which heated Virginia homes at that time were a gathering place for drinking, conversation, and cheerful evenings of all kinds. With this thought in mind, the officials of Williamsburg feel it fitting and proper to include both the Yule Log Ceremony and the Wassail Bowl in celebrating today's Christmas holidays.

VIRGINIA PEANUT SOUP
(King's Arms Tavern Cream of Peanut Soup)

    1 *small onion, chopped*
    1 *rib celery, very finely chopped*
    2 *tablespoons butter*
    1¹/₂ *tablespoons flour*
    4 *cups chicken stock (or canned chicken broth)*
    1 *cup smooth peanut butter*
    1 *cup light cream*
    Peanuts, chopped (optional)

Sauté the onion and celery in the butter over a low flame until soft, but do not allow them to brown. Stir in the flour until well blended. Add the chicken stock gradually, stirring constantly, and bring to a boil. Simmer 5 minutes. Remove from heat, strain, and rub what remains through a sieve or put through a food processor with a small amount of the liquid.

Place the peanut butter in a bowl and add the liquid gradually, blending well so no lumps form. Stir in the cream. Pour into a saucepan and place over low heat. Heat, but do not boil. Serve garnished with chopped peanuts if desired. This soup is also good served ice cold.

MAKES 8 SERVINGS

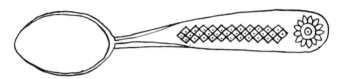

WILLIAMSBURG SPOON BREAD
(Christiana Campbell's Tavern Spoon Bread)

1 1/2 *teaspoons sugar*
1 *teaspoon salt*
1 *cup cornmeal*
4 *tablespoons butter*
1 1/3 *cups boiling water*
3 *eggs*
1 *tablespoon baking powder*
1 1/3 *cups hot milk*

Preheat the oven at 350° . Grease a 2-quart casserole. Mix the sugar and salt with the cornmeal and blend well. Add the butter and pour in the boiling water, stirring constantly, until the butter melts. Allow to cool.

Beat the eggs with the baking powder until very light and fluffy, then add to the cornmeal mixture. Stir in the milk and pour into the prepared casserole. Place the casserole in a shallow pan of hot water and bake for 35 to 40 minutes. Serve hot, spooning out portions.

MAKES 8 OR MORE SERVINGS

TIPSY SQUIRE
(Old Richmond Sponge Cake Recipe, with Modern Measurements)

10 *eggs*
2 *cups sugar*
Juice and grated rind of 1 lemon
2 *teaspoons vanilla extract*
$2^{1}/_{4}$ *cups flour*
$^{1}/_{2}$ *teaspoon salt*

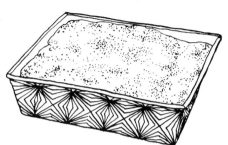

Preheat the oven at 325°. Separate the eggs and beat the yolks until very thick. Add the sugar gradually and continue beating until very thick. Add the lemon juice and grated rind and vanilla extract. Sift the flour and salt and add to the batter about half at a time, mixing gently but well. Beat the egg whites until stiff but not dry, and fold into the batter gently but thoroughly. Turn into two well-greased and floured 8-inch-square baking pans. Bake 30 minutes, or until cake tester inserted in the center comes out clean. Turn out on wire racks to cool.

FOR FILLING AND FINISHING:

Sherry
2 *packages vanilla pudding prepared according to package directions (or 1 quart homemade vanilla custard)*
$1^{1}/_{2}$ *cups split or slivered blanched almonds*
$1^{1}/_{2}$ *cups heavy cream*
1 *cup chopped toasted almonds*

Cut the cooled cakes horizontally through centers. Sprinkle sherry very generously over all cut sides. Put the sections back together, place on plate, cover, and refrigerate.

Prepare the packaged vanilla pudding or homemade vanilla custard and chill well.

Cut each cake into 9 squares.* Place 1 square on each individual serving dish. Spoon the vanilla custard over each square. (If using packaged pudding, stir the pudding well before spoon-

---

* If the cakes are left whole and the balance of the recipe is prepared as above, the recipe is then called Tipsy Cake.

ing over the cake.) Place a second square of cake over the custard. Sprinkle with split or slivered blanched almonds. Spoon the remaining custard over the almonds. Whip the cream until stiff and spoon over the top of each dessert. Sprinkle with chopped toasted almonds.

MAKES 18 SERVINGS†

SALLY LUNN
(King's Arms Tavern)

1 cup milk
$^1/_2$ cup shortening
$^1/_4$ cup water
4 cups sifted flour
$^1/_3$ cup sugar
2 teaspoons salt
2 packages active dry yeast
3 eggs

Heat the milk, shortening, and water until very warm, about 120°. The shortening does not need to melt. Blend $1^1/_3$ cups of the flour, the sugar, salt, and yeast in a large mixing bowl. Blend the warm liquid into the flour mixture. Beat with an electric mixer at medium speed about 2 minutes, scraping the sides of the bowl occasionally. Gradually add $^2/_3$ cup more flour and the eggs and beat at high speed for 2 minutes. Add the remaining 2 cups of flour and mix well. The batter will be thick, but not stiff.

Cover and let rise in a warm place until double in bulk, about $1^1/_4$ hours. Grease heavily a 10-inch tube cake pan or a bundt pan. Beat the dough down with a spatula or at the lowest speed on an electric mixer and turn into the prepared pan. Cover and let rise in a warm place until increased in bulk one-third to one-half, about 15 to 30 minutes.

---

†If you wish to make only 9 servings, you may freeze one of the cakes for another time, make only 1 pint of vanilla pudding or custard, and reduce the amount of almonds and heavy cream by half.

Preheat the oven at 350°, 10 minutes before the Sally Lunn is ready to be baked. Bake 35 to 45 minutes. Run a knife around the center and outer edges of the bread and turn it onto a plate to cool.

MAKES 10 OR MORE SERVINGS

WILLIAMSBURG HOLIDAY COOKIES

¹/₂ cup butter
1 cup sugar
1 egg, beaten
1 teaspoon vanilla extract
1 tablespoon heavy cream
2 cups sifted flour
1¹/₂ teaspoons baking powder
¹/₂ teaspoon salt
Colored sugar

Cream the butter and add the sugar gradually. Add the egg, vanilla extract, and heavy cream, and mix well. Sift together and add the flour, baking powder, and salt, mix well, cover, and chill in the refrigerator for several hours.

Preheat the oven at 350°. Roll out the dough on a lightly floured board and cut into circles or fancy shapes. Sprinkle with colored sugar and arrange on greased baking sheets. Bake about 7 minutes. If cookies are not served immediately, store in a covered jar to retain crispness.

MAKES ABOUT 4 DOZEN MEDIUM-SIZED COOKIES

WASSAIL BOWL

$^1/_2$ cup water
1 cup sugar
2 sticks cinnamon
3 slices lemon
2 cups cranberry juice
2 cups lemon juice, strained
4 cups red wine
Lemon slices

Boil the water, sugar, cinnamon sticks, and 3 slices of lemon together for about 5 minutes to make a spicy syrup. Strain. Heat but do not boil the cranberry juice, lemon juice, and red wine. Add the syrup to the hot cranberry mixture. Pour into a bowl, decorate with lemon slices, and serve piping hot in punch cups. The Wassail Bowl can also be laced with brandy if desired.

MAKES ABOUT 20 SERVINGS

Festival Facts

Colonial Williamsburg, a nonprofit educational organization, is open to the public 365 days of the year. For those unfamiliar with Williamsburg, it will be of interest to know that it was originally built in 1699 as the new capital of the Virginia Colony and was, as such, a cultural and political center for many years. The historic area of today's Williamsburg covers 173 acres of the original town and utilizes the original mile-long street plan. In the center area are eighty-eight preserved and restored houses, shops, taverns, and public buildings, and an additional fifty major buildings and many smaller structures have also been rebuilt on their original sites. Williamsburg is on U.S. 60 in southeastern Virginia. For further details about Christmas and other special events, write: The Colonial Williamsburg Foundation, Williamsburg, Virginia 23185.

Junior Baking Contest of The Association of Connecticut Fairs

10

From the New York City commuting communities of Fairfield County to the rural villages in the Berkshire foothills of Litchfield County and the old coastal and river towns of New London and Middlesex counties, agricultural fairs are held by the dozens every summer and fall throughout the state of Connecticut. Despite its population density, prevalence of bedroom communities, and industrialization of cities, a good part of Connecticut remains rural, with crop and livestock farms providing thriving livelihoods for many of its residents.

Whether they live on farms or in towns or cities, Connecticutites flock to their country fairs, town fairs, community fairs, county fairs, Grange fairs, 4-H fairs, horse fairs, and state fairs to see and participate in many activities they cherish. Even though industrial and commercial exhibits often outnumber the agricultural ones at these events nowadays, it's still standing room only for the farm animal team-pulling contests, harness and saddle horse shows, wood-chopping demonstrations, fish and game shows, prize-awarding shows of cattle, hogs, horses, sheep, goats, rabbits, and poultry, and exhibits of farm machinery.

Exhibits of handsome vegetables, fruits, and flowers, fancy work, canning, preserving, and baking abound, particularly at the Grange and 4-H fairs. There's a lively competition for the rather modest prizes offered in the many contests held at these fairs, indicating that people simply enjoy taking part in the activities. Contests range from photography to baby health, woodcutting, fiddling, pie eating, cooking, and baking.

Two enthusiastically entered contests at many of the fifty-six fairs sponsored by the Association of Connecticut Fairs are the Baking Contest and the Junior Baking Contest. The first-prize winner in each of these categories at each fair is eligible to participate in the final competition at the end of the season after all the fairs have been held. Girls and boys aged fifteen years or younger enter the Junior Baking Contest by following the contest rules and submitting their example of the year's chosen recipe.

Sour Cream Girls, which are doll-shaped cookies, was the recipe used in one of the Junior Baking Contests. Each of the thirty-seven finalists presented four of his or her best cookies for judging. The "girls" were adorned with such diverse decorations as silver balls, colored shot, M&M candies, almond slivers, and icings of every color. They sported licorice braids and eyelashes, smiling red gumdrop mouths, and unwinking blue-frosted eyes. Some were decorated as angels, and others as apron-wearing schoolgirls, but all had obviously been made with a good deal of thought and care. Although they're important, decorations alone don't determine winners in any of the contests. The judges of the Junior Baking Contest carefully taste and note the texture, flavor, general outside appearance, and shape of every entrant's cookies, and rate them by a detailed point-score system.

First-prize winner of the contest featuring Sour Cream Girls

was Dennis Borovy, Jr., from Torrington, Connecticut, who sur-
passed his honorable-mention-winning sister, Dennise, and his
second-place-winning sister, Dawn, to become the best Junior
Baker for the second time in three years. His winning cookies had
raisin eyes, walnut noses, and cherry-slice mouths and wore pink-
flowerette-frosted dresses with colored-shot-sprinkled bodices.

Recipes for both the well-flavored Sour Cream Girls and a
previous year's contest choice, thick, hearty Gingerbread Boys,
follow.

SOUR CREAM GIRLS

1/2 cup shortening
2 cups sugar
3 eggs
1 cup sour cream
2 teaspoons vanilla extract
4 1/4 cups sifted flour
1 tablespoon baking soda
1 teaspoon baking powder
1/2 teaspoon salt
1 teaspoon nutmeg

Cream the shortening, add the sugar, and mix well. Add
the eggs and beat until light. Stir in the sour cream and vanilla
extract. Sift together and add the flour, baking soda, baking
powder, salt, and nutmeg. Mix until well blended. Cover and refrigerate for 3 hours or overnight.

Preheat the oven at 375°. Roll out the dough, about one-
fourth at a time, on a well-floured board to a thickness of about
1/4 inch. Using the outer part of a doughnut cutter, cut circles for
bodies. Using the center part of a doughnut cutter, cut small
circles for heads. For each girl, cut a narrow strip from two sides
of a large circle, leaving a triangular-shaped piece for the body.
Place the narrow strips at the sides for arms, and use a small circle
for the head. Place on ungreased cookie sheets 2 inches apart.

Decorate the cookies with raisins, candies, candied fruits, or

any appropriate edible decoration. Bake 10 to 12 minutes.
Cool on a wire rack, and decorate with icing if desired.

MAKES ABOUT 6 DOZEN

The following recipe, while not provided by the Association of Connecticut Fairs, is a good and easy-to-work-with decorating icing for the cookies. Apply it to the girls with small watercolor brushes, allowing each color to dry before applying another color over it.

Icing

½ cup sifted confectioner's sugar
2 teaspoons water
1 or 2 drops vegetable coloring

Combine the confectioner's sugar with the water in a small cup. Add the vegetable coloring and mix well. Repeat the entire process for the number of colors needed. You'll probably want a portion each of red, yellow, blue, green, uncolored white, and one or two additional colors. If the icing is too stiff, add more water. If too runny, add more sifted confectioner's sugar. Paint and decorate the features and clothing of the girls as you like, adding silver balls, colored sprinkles, or chocolate shot if desired.

GINGERBREAD BOYS

⅓ cup shortening
1 cup brown sugar, firmly packed
1½ cups dark molasses
⅔ cup cold water
7 cups sifted flour
2 teaspoons baking soda
1 teaspoon salt
1 teaspoon allspice
1 teaspoon ginger
1 teaspoon cloves
1 teaspoon cinnamon

Cream the shortening until soft. Add the brown sugar and molasses and mix well. Stir in the water. Sift together and add the flour, baking soda, salt, allspice, ginger, cloves, and cinnamon. Place in the refrigerator 2 hours or in the freezer 30 minutes.

Preheat the oven at 350°. On a floured board, roll out the dough $^1/_2$-inch thick. Use a floured gingerbread-boy cutter measuring 5x3$^1/_2$ inches to cut out the cookies. With a pancake turner, transfer carefully to a greased baking sheet. Decorate with raisins, bits of candied cherries, gumdrops, or any other eatable item. Cookies may also be frosted with decorating icing when cool.

Bake about 15 minutes until no imprint remains when touched lightly with a finger. Cool slightly, then carefully remove from the baking sheet.

MAKES 1 TO 1$^1/_2$ DOZEN COOKIES

Festival Facts

The following are the major Connecticut fairs held from July to October: North Stonington, Connecticut Agricultural, Lebanon Country, Hamburg, Bridgewater Country, Chester, Brooklyn, Goshen, Woodstock, Haddam Neck, North Haven, Hebron Harvest, Portland Agricultural, Terryville Country, Bethlehem, Four Town, Guilford, Durham Agricultural, Berlin, Danbury, Harwinton, and Riverton. For further information on these and other Connecticut fairs, write: Mrs. Edward Mendelson, Secretary, The Association of Connecticut Fairs, 30 Todd Drive, North Haven, Connecticut 06473.

Danish Days

11

Solvang, California

The travel folders say, quite accurately, that Solvang, California, is like a page from Hans Christian Andersen. Some call the town Little Denmark, U.S.A., for it's so genuinely Scandinavian that even the service stations and the post office have been built in typical Danish thatched-roof style, as have all the other buildings. Windmills grace the landscape, gas streetlights imported from Copenhagen glow at night in the center of town, and white storks perch on the rooftops, nesting near the chimneys as do their European counterparts across the sea. True, they are artificial storks, since the real birds don't live in this hemisphere, but they are charming to see, and the residents enjoy perpetuating the belief that a stork on the roof brings good luck to the household below.

Solvang, as one might guess, was settled entirely by Danish people. A group of Danish educators from the Midwest started the town early in this century after searching for a site on which to establish a Danish-type folk school and to carry on the customs and arts of the Danes. They fashioned their town, whose name means "sunny field," like one that might be found in Denmark, even including a Little Mermaid statue in the town square like the original in Copenhagen's Langelinie Park. The town never became large, but although it has a population of only about two thousand today, Solvang entertains over a million and a quarter tourists annually. People come every day to see the unique town, and at any time of the year one can go on a tour of Solvang in a motorized version of the type of streetcar that was used in Copenhagen before the turn of the century, or listen to the Danish band playing in the town park, or stop at one of the bakery shops and choose from myriads of Danish pastries which can be sampled on the spot at conveniently located tables. There are special festivities at the beginning of Lent, and at Christmastime the buildings of Solvang are lit from dormer to doorway with thousands of festive lights.

But the high point of the year is a two-day September festival called Danish Days which attracts people (many of Danish extraction) from all over the nation who come to see the residents don native costumes, watch the dancers do old-time Danish folk dances, the singers entertain with Danish songs, and the equestrian teams do battle in Danish spear ring riding. Children are entertained with a fairy-tale hour in Hans Christian Andersen Park, would-be travelers wishfully watch Danish travel movies, and everyone sees a parade, dances at the Danish Ball, and eats Danish treats from morning until night.

All this is possible because of the efforts of Solvang's many families of Danish heritage who make Danish Days a really special time. Mrs. Cora Tarnow, for example, who has supplied the official aebleskiver and other recipes below, has grown up with the town and was instrumental in the birth of the Danish Days celebration. Her entire family helps in the preparation of aebleskiver, her husband is director of the Junior Gymnasts, her daughter sings in the roving chorus, her three granddaughters take part in the dancing and musical productions—one having been "Danish Maid" one year—and her son-in-law, Johames Jaeger, has built many of the handsome windmills and other buildings seen about the town.

Visitors line up early in the morning to be seated for the unusual Aebleskiver Breakfast. The center of town is converted into an outdoor kitchen and restaurant, with row upon row of aebleskiver pans being tended by Solvang men and women who take great delight and pride in making the famous Danish pancake. Aebleskiver means "apple pancake balls," and originally the pancakes had a slice of apple or a bit of applesauce in them. However, since the apple has a tendency to leak out and soil the pan, it's impractical from a pan-washing point of view to cook apples in the pancakes during festival times. The pancakes, which are nevertheless apple shaped, are delicious with or without apples, and are made in iron skillets called, curiously, "monk's pans." Each pan has seven cup-shaped depressions into which the batter is poured. The aebleskiver are then poked and turned with a knitting needle until they become puffed, round, and browned, at which point they are served, five to a person, with jam, Danish sausage or bacon, fruit juice, and hot Danish coffee.

The California sun becomes too hot for serving food "on the streets" in the afternoon, so those who are ready for more good Danish food can stop at lunchtime in one of the many eating places about town for Dansk smorrebrod, Danish open-face sandwiches. Richly buttered dark bread, either rye or pumpernickel, which forms the base of these tempting creations, is completely obscured from sight when piled high with savory fillings of meat, fish, eggs, or cheese, and artfully trimmed with various garnishes. The sandwiches are always eaten with a knife and fork, for they are too laden to be handled with the fingers. Some favorite sandwich combinations are roast pork with pickled beets and red cabbage, liver pâté with pickled beets and cucumber salad, hard-cooked egg slices with lettuce and herring tidbits or anchovies, smoked eel with scrambled egg, Danish or Swiss cheese with lettuce and radishes, shrimp with mayonnaise, and Danish salami with onion and meat jelly.

Midafternoon coffee and a bit of Danish pastry are a must with Solvang people during Danish Days as well as all other days. The bakeries offer a variety of cookies, buns, pastries, pretzels, and little cakes which they are happy to sell in a "one-of-this-and-one-of-that" fashion in order that visitors may have a well-rounded sampling of their wares.

After watching or participating in an afternoon dancing contest on the outdoor stage, seeing the Junior Gymnasts or bicycle spear ring riders perform, and poking about in the town shops, it's time for yet another Danish meal. A good choice for dinner at one of the many restaurants open during Danish Days is det store kolde bord, which translates to "the large cold table" in English and "smorgasbord" in Swedish. A typical table would include various kinds of fish (pickled herring tidbits, herring salad, lobster salad, shrimp salad, anchovies, matjes herring, sardines, fish balls, and warm fish fillets), a selection of meats (baked ham, meatballs, roast pork, roast beef, frikadeller, liver pâté, rolled veal, and jellied veal), countless salads and vegetables (potato salad, cucumber salad, aspics, red cabbage, pickled beets, pickled cucumber, filled tomatoes, olives, radishes), and a variety of breads (pumpernickel, white bread, flatbread, sourdough, rye, whole wheat, and rye crisp). For those who'd rather sit and be served, a favorite Danish dinner is frikadeller (Danish meatballs) with rod kaal (red cabbage), followed by a serving of traditional unbaked Danish apple cake—this time really made with apples.

The recipes which follow are for Danish Days Aebleskiver (pancakes), Dansk Smorrebrod (Danish open-face sandwiches), Rugbrod (rye bread perfect for making Danish open-face sandwiches), Leverpostej (liver pâté also perfect for Danish open-face sandwiches), Kraemmerhuse (pastry cones filled with whipped cream to be eaten with afternoon coffee), Frikadeller (meatballs), Rod Kaal (red cabbage), and Aeblekage (Danish apple cake).

AEBLESKIVER
(Danish Pancakes)

In order to make aebleskiver properly, use either a Danish aebleskiver pan, Dutch poffertjes pan, Swedish plattar pan, or any heavy skillet-type pan which has rounded depressions into which batter can be poured. Pans of this type can be bought at hardware stores, shops selling imported wares, and gourmet cookware shops.

4 eggs, separated
1 tablespoon sugar
4 cups biscuit mix (such as Bisquick)
1 teaspoon salt
2¹/₂ cups milk
Melted butter or margarine

Beat the egg yolks well with the sugar. Sift together and add the biscuit mix and salt. Add the milk gradually and mix until smooth. Beat the egg whites until stiff and fold into the batter.

Place the aebleskiver pan over medium heat. Pour 1 teaspoon melted butter or margarine in each depression, and tilt the pan to distribute it evenly. Fill the depressions almost to the top with batter, and cook, turning with a knitting needle or icepick, until puffed and browned all over. Lower the heat if the pan becomes too hot during cooking. Put butter in the depressions for each batch.

Put 5 aebleskiver on each serving dish. If desired, sprinkle with sifted confectioner's sugar and serve with jam. May be served for dessert, or with sausage or bacon for breakfast, lunch, or late supper.

MAKES ABOUT 50 AEBLESKIVER, OR 10 SERVINGS

DANSK SMORREBROD
(Danish Open-Face Sandwiches)

Slice Rugbrod rye bread; (recipe follows), pumpernickel, or
any dark bread thinly, butter well, and cover generously with one
or two foods from the following list. The bread may be cut in half
if desired. Arrange the fillings attractively, folding or layering
them evenly and/or alternating the foods in interesting ways.

Pickled herring
Liver pâté (recipe follows)
Roast pork
Roast beef
Shrimps
Frikadeller (recipe follows)
Sliced ham
Rolled veal
Smoked salmon
Tongue
Salami
Sardines
Warm fish fillets
Smoked eel
Lobster
Fried liver
Bacon
Roast duck

Cheese (Danish, blue, or Swiss)
Herring salad (Mix together $^1/_2$ cup whipped cream, 2 ta-
    blespoons vinegar, 1 teaspoon sugar, salt and pepper to
    taste, 1 small chopped onion, 1 small peeled, chopped
    apple, and 1 cup pickled herring tidbits)
Curry salad (Mix together $^1/_2$ cup each pickled herring tid-
    bits, small-sized cooked macaroni, and mayonnaise, and
    1 chopped, hard-cooked egg, 1 teaspoon curry powder,
    and salt and pepper to taste)
Italian salad (Mix together equal quantities of cooked peas,
    cooked carrots, and cooked small-sized macaroni, and

moisten with mayonnaise, adding salt and pepper to taste)

Decorate the open-face sandwiches with any of the items from the following list. The vegetables and pickles can be trimmed, cut into interesting shapes, twisted into curves, and so on.

Onion rings
Chopped onion
Fried onions
Pickled beets
Red cabbage (recipe follows)
Chopped egg
Scrambled egg
Whole raw egg yolk
Anchovies
Jellied consommé
Chives
Parsley
Dill
Lettuce
Radishes
Tomato slices
Fried mushrooms
Pickles
Olives

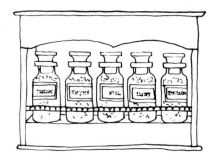

Currant jelly
Lingonberries (bottled)
Mayonnaise (pipe through fancy tube if desired)
Rémoulade sauce
Tartare sauce

RUGBROD
(Rye Bread for Danish Open-Face Sandwiches)

2 packages active dry yeast
$^1/_2$ cup warm water (about 115°)
1 teaspoon sugar
1$^1/_2$ teaspoons salt
2 tablespoons caraway seeds
1 tablespoon melted butter
6 cups rye flour
2 cups all-purpose flour
3 cups buttermilk
Melted butter

In a large bowl stir the yeast with warm water and sugar until the yeast dissolves. Set in a warm place for 5 to 10 minutes, until it starts to become foamy. Add the salt, caraway seeds, and melted butter. Sift together the rye and all-purpose flours and add alternately with the buttermilk. Mix well and knead thoroughly. Place in a greased bowl, grease the top of the dough, cover with a dish towel or plastic wrap, and let it rise in a warm place until doubled in bulk, 1$^1/_2$ to 2$^1/_2$ hours.

Turn the dough onto a lightly floured board, knead lightly, and divide it into two equal portions. Shape into loaves and place in two 5x9-inch greased loaf pans. Cover and let rise again in a warm place until doubled in bulk. Brush the loaf tops with melted butter and bake in a preheated 400° oven 45 to 50 minutes. Remove from the pans and cool on a wire rack.

MAKES 2 LOAVES

LEVERPOSTEJ
(Liver Pâté)

2 *tablespoons butter*
2 *tablespoons flour*
1 *cup milk*
1 *pound pork liver, cut into pieces*
$^1/_2$ *pound pork fat or fatback, cut into pieces*
1 *medium onion, coarsely chopped*
2 *eggs*
1 *teaspoon salt*
$^1/_2$ *teaspoon pepper*
$^1/_2$ *teaspoon ground allspice*
Bacon or thin slices fatback

Melt the butter in a saucepan and stir in the flour. Cook, stirring, until smooth. Add the milk and cook over medium heat, stirring with a wire whisk, until thickened and smooth. Remove from the heat and cool.

Meanwhile, put the pork liver, pork fat or fatback, and onion through a food processor or through a meat grinder three or four times, using a medium blade. Set aside.

When the sauce has cooled to lukewarm, beat in the eggs, salt, pepper, and allspice. Combine with the liver mixture.

Blanch enough bacon or thin slices of fatback to line the bottom and sides of a 5x9-inch loaf pan, allowing enough extra slices to cover the top of the pan before baking. Pat the bacon or fatback dry with paper towels and line the pan. Pour in the pâté mixture. Lay slices of bacon or fatback over the top of the pâté.

Preheat the oven at 350°. Set the loaf pan in a larger pan and pour boiling water all around to a depth halfway up the sides of the loaf pan. Place in the oven and bake 1$^1/_2$ hours. Set the loaf pan on a wire rack to cool, but do not unmold. Cover with aluminum foil and place a heavy weight on top. When it is cool enough to handle, refrigerate with the weight still on top. Keep refrigerated 24 hours before serving.

If using it for open-face sandwiches, slice the pâté thinly and garnish with pickled beets, pickled cucumbers, and a slice of jellied consommé.   MAKES 1 LOAF

KRAEMMERHUSE
(Cones with Whipped Cream)

2 eggs
$^1/_2$ cup sugar
$^1/_4$ teaspoon salt
$^2/_3$ cup sifted flour
1 cup heavy cream
Currant or raspberry jelly

Preheat the oven at 375°. Beat the eggs until thick. Add the sugar and salt and continue beating until thick and lemon-colored. Stir in the flour. Drop the dough onto a well-greased baking sheet, a tablespoonful at a time, spacing well apart. Do not bake more than four at a time. Spread the dough out with a spatula. Bake 5 minutes, or until lightly browned around the edges.

Remove from the oven and pick up the cookies with a spatula one at a time, shaping each one immediately into a cone shape with the fingers. The cookies will not be too hot or difficult to handle, but must be shaped quickly. Place them seam side down on a wire rack to cool. Continue baking on cooled baking sheets until the dough has been used up.

At serving time, beat the heavy cream until very stiff. Fill the cones with whipped cream and decorate with a bit of currant or raspberry jelly. Serve immediately.

MAKES ABOUT 20

Kraemmerhuse are good with afternoon coffee or as a dessert.

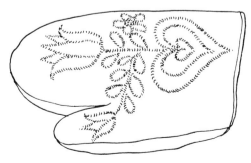

FRIKADELLER
(Danish Meatballs)

1 *pound lean beef*
$^1/_2$ *pound lean pork*
$^1/_4$ *cup flour*
1 *teaspoon salt*
Pepper to taste
1 *onion, grated*
2 *eggs*
1 *cup milk*
Butter or margarine

Have the butcher put the beef and pork through the meat grinder twice, or grind it yourself several times. Combine with the flour, salt, pepper, and onion, and mix well. Add the eggs, one at a time, combining well. Add the milk and mix well. Form into meatballs and fry in a skillet in butter or margarine.

MAKES ABOUT 16

Frikadeller may be baked in a loaf pan as a meat loaf, rather than as meatballs. In either case, serve with Rod Kaal (red cabbage; recipe below).

ROD KAAL
(Red Cabbage)

1 *three-pound head red cabbage*
2 *tablespoons vinegar*
$^1/_4$ *cup butter, melted*
$^1/_4$ *cup sugar*
1 *teaspoon salt*
1 *apple, peeled, cored, and cubed*
$^1/_2$ *cup currant jelly (or currant juice)*

Cut the cabbage into quarters and remove the core. Chop the cabbage fine and sprinkle it with vinegar to prevent darkening. Melt the butter in a large skillet. Stir in the sugar and salt. Add the cabbage and toss well. Cook 15 minutes, tossing occasionally. Add the apple and currant jelly or juice, and toss well. Cover and simmer slowly about 2 hours, tossing once or twice during cooking.

Serve as a vegetable or as a garnish on open-face sandwiches.

AEBLEKAGE
(Apple Cake)

1 1/2 cups rusk crumbs (1 four-ounce package)
2 tablespoons sugar
1/4 cup butter
6 to 8 medium-sized almond macaroons
2 to 4 tablespoons sherry
3 cups thick applesauce
3/4 cup heavy cream, whipped
Currant jelly

Brown the rusk crumbs, sugar, and butter in a skillet over low heat, stirring constantly. Remove from heat and cool.

In the bottom of a glass serving bowl, place the macaroons, and sprinkle with as much of the sherry as they will absorb. Put alternate layers of the applesauce and the crumb mixture over the macaroons. Decorate the top with whipped cream and little dots of currant jelly. The dish may be served immediately or chilled before serving.

MAKES 8 SERVINGS

Festival Facts

Danish Days, which began in 1952, occurs on a weekend after mid-September in Solvang, California, which is on the southern fork of Route 154, about forty-five miles north of Santa Barbara via U.S. 101. For further information, write: Danish Days, % Chamber of Commerce, Solvang, California 93463.

National Date Festival

12

Indio, California

Abbada, Khadrawy, Medjhul, Zahidi. If these names conjure up visions of Arabian Nights, well they should, for they're names of some of the date varieties ranging from jet-black soft dates to huge twelve-to-the-pound reddish-brown ones that were originally brought in from the Middle East and now grow in the heart of California's Coachella Valley. In Indio, in the midst of this major date-producing area of the western hemisphere, one of America's more unusual festivals takes place annually for ten days, celebrating the date harvest and bringing to life the magic and mystery of ancient Baghdad, complete with camels, dancing girls, and dates by the millions.

While camels can live quite nicely on a diet of date meal and water, and nomadic tribesmen of Arabia are said to thrive on eating only dates and milk, there is more variety and just as many dates in store for visitors to Indio's National Date Festival, including endless date sweetmeats, delicious date ice creams, and date milk shakes. For those unschooled in the forms in which dates can be bought, it's a revelation to learn that there are many tantalizing and useful date products to be had. Date butter, for instance, or creamed dates are sold for use as a spread or for making blender drinks; date sugar granules, which contain minerals and a lower calorie count than other sugars, can be used in any way one would normally use sugar; date chips, which are dehydrated date pieces, can be eaten as snacks or used in cooking; and packaged pitted, chopped dates are ready for instant use in baking, on cereals, in salads, and whatnot.

Hungry festival-goers can eat their dates or picnic foods seated under the date palms, go to the indoor/outdoor Caravansary, or have a bite or a date goody at one of the many food concessions on the fairgrounds. There are mammoth date displays and exhibits of date products, so one can see firsthand how dates grow on the palm in huge clusters.

Date growers and packers who display their wares at the festival are happy to tell you that dates are one of the most unusual and expensive crops to produce. They point out that dates grow forty-eight female to one male palm per acre (perhaps inspiring the idea of harem life in the desert world of old), require dethorning about fifteen times a year by workers who also scoot up and down the trunks endless times to cut out old branches, pollinate the new blossoms (which grow inconveniently at the very tops of the trees), and harvest the annual crop, and that in spite of its being a desert plant, the date palm requires vast amounts of water to keep its root structure soaking wet at all times. It's interesting to note that if you plant a date seed, you'll get a new kind of date tree every time. To perpetuate a variety of dates, then, they must be propagated by planting offshoots of the palm itself. Offshoots grow near the true bases during the first ten or fifteen years of life of the trees.

Strictly for fun, one mustn't miss the camel races held daily during the festival. These denizens of the desert roar around the track ridden by either men or women who prod the animals on with riding crops in some of the most unpredictable races to be found anywhere this side of the Sahara. In the same arena there are also daily races for ostriches not given to hiding their heads in the sand. The giant birds are harnessed to sulkies much like harness-racing horses, and are guided by sheik-costumed riders who urge on their high-stepping charges with brooms and shouts to produce a winner.

Other entertainments include free nightly *Arabian Nights* pageants featuring tales of Scheherazade performed by dozens of singers, actors, and dancers; an Arabian street parade; and the Magic Land of Aladdin, which combines live performers with puppets and magic.

Then there's a gems and minerals show, said to be one of the nation's largest, livestock auctions, a photographic salon, a petting zoo, a carnival midway, and commercial and industrial exhibits. There are also an old-time country cooking demonstration, and cooking competitions among the Senior Home Arts Department and Future Farmers of America Department, who bring in their baked goods and confections for judging. The 4-H Club has a Date Cooking Contest, and their various groups cook right at the festival for all to see. Recipes of some recent winners of the contest are given below, including a rich Date Nut Torte baked by Michelle Riffle of the Black and White Ponies, and tasty Cinnamon Date Nut Cookies baked by Joanne Dodson of the Ramona Rancheros. Recipes for a tempting Date Milk Shake and Date Ice Cream as sold at the festival are also included.

DATE NUT TORTE

2 *eggs*
1 *cup sugar*
$^1/_2$ *cup sifted flour*
3 *teaspoons vanilla extract*
1 *cup chopped nuts*
$1^1/_2$ *cups chopped dates*

Preheat the oven at 325°. Beat the eggs lightly. Beat in the sugar. Stir in the sifted flour. Add the vanilla extract, nuts, and dates, and mix well. Turn into a greased 9-inch-square baking pan. Bake 30 minutes. Cool on a wire rack. Cut into squares.

MAKES 9 OR 16

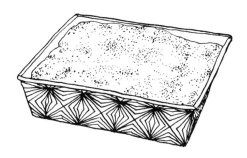

CINNAMON DATE NUT COOKIES

3/4 cup margarine
2 cups brown sugar, firmly packed
1 1/2 teaspoons cinnamon
1 teaspoon vanilla extract
1/2 teaspoon salt
2 eggs
1 teaspoon baking soda
1/2 cup boiling water
2 cups flour
3 cups quick oats
1/2 cup chopped nuts
1 1/2 cups finely chopped dates

Preheat the oven at 325°. Cream the margarine and add the sugar, beating until smooth. Add the cinnamon, vanilla extract, salt, and eggs, and beat again. Dissolve the baking soda in the boiling water and add alternately with the flour and quick oats. Stir in the nuts and chopped dates. Drop by generous teaspoonsful on ungreased baking sheets and bake about 12 minutes.

MAKES 6 TO 7 DOZEN

DATE MILK SHAKE

¹/₂ cup milk
¹/₂ cup chopped dates, loosely packed
1 tablespoon honey
¹/₂ pint vanilla ice cream

Whirl milk, dates, and honey in a blender until the dates are pulverized. Add the ice cream and whirl briefly. Pour into a large glass.

MAKES 1 SERVING

DATE ICE CREAM

²/₃ cup pitted dates, firmly packed
2 tablespoons honey
1 quart vanilla ice cream

Grind together the dates and honey, using the medium blade of a grinder, or put through a food processor. Soften the ice cream in a bowl with a wooden spoon and stir in the date-honey mixture. Pack into a plastic container, cover, and refreeze until firm.

MAKES ABOUT 1 QUART

Festival Facts

The National Date Festival, which began in 1935, is held annually for ten days in mid-February at the Fairgrounds, Highway 111 and Arabia Street, Indio, California. For further information, write: National Date Festival, P.O. Drawer NNNN, Indio, California 92201.

Duluth Folk Festival

13

Duluth, Minnesota

What started as a summer garden party on the lawn of a private house in Duluth some thirty years ago grew and blossomed into a full-scale folk festival attended by nine to twelve thousand people annually, and requiring a place as large as the city's Leif Erikson Park in which to display the many foods and handcrafts of the citizenry.

The early settlers of Duluth were predominantly Scandinavian, and some of the ethnic markets at the festival represent the many Finnish, Swedish, and Norwegian people who still live in the city. But there are also booths manned by the area's original inhabitants, American Indians, as well as those of Afro-Americans, Mexicans, Israelis, Filipinos, Greeks, Syrians, Yugoslavians, Britons, Poles, Germans, Italians, and Chinese. While not every group participates every year, there are at least a dozen who do, offering their most mouth-watering treats to festival guests.

It would be hard to say which food is the uncontested festival favorite, but there are a few that always seem to draw goodly crowds—patica (or povitica), a luscious nut-and-honey-filled pastry of Yugoslavia, Polish sausage made by a local Polish merchant, Greek pastries sold by the piece for instant nibbling or by the box for at-home enjoyment, and Indian fry bread. Mrs. John Radosevich, chairman of the festival's Yugoslavian Ethnic Market, has supplied her recipe for Patica, and the recipe for a Finnish specialty, Maksalaalikko, a beautifully seasoned rice-and-liver casserole, has been given by Nellie Hakanson of the Finnish Ethnic Market.

The city of Duluth, sitting on the shores of Lake Superior about 150 miles north of St. Paul, quite deservedly considers itself the educational and cultural center of northern Minnesota. It has two colleges, including a medical school, a community theater dating back to 1914, a ballet company, a symphony orchestra, and prospering arts and crafts communities. The cultural interests of the people are reflected in the caliber and diversification of the exhibits and booths at the Duluth Folk Festival. In addition to the ethnic foods and artifacts, there's a book market to browse through, a thieves' market in which to search for a bit of jewelry, household gimcrack, or art object, a plant booth, a bazaar, a Simple Living Display, a large arts and crafts section, a Head of the Lakes World Affairs Council and United Nations Organization booth, and a special children's fair with a fish pond, balloons, sno-cones, cotton candy, and puppet shows.

Entertainment is equally varied throughout the day, with Italians dancing the tarantella, the Bahai religious group, whose membership is international, presenting its New Day Singers, groups of Spanish, Greek, Tahitian, Russian, and many other dancers doing their own special steps, a band expertly performing under a grant from the recording industries, and a Parade of Nations for one and all to march in.

PATICA (OR POVITICA)

FOR THE FILLING:
1 *pound ground walnuts*
2 *eggs*
2 *cups milk*
1 *cup sugar*
1 *cup honey*
1 *teaspoon cinnamon (optional)*

FOR THE DOUGH:
1 *package active dry yeast (or 1 yeast cake)*
2 *tablespoons warm water (about 115°)*
$^1/_2$ *teaspoon sugar*
$^1/_2$ *cup sugar*
$^1/_2$ *cup melted butter*
1 *teaspoon salt*
1 *cup boiling water*
2 *eggs, beaten*
5 *cups flour*

FOR THE FILLING: Combine the walnuts, eggs, milk, sugar, and honey in a heavy saucepan or in the top of a double boiler over hot water. Cook over low heat, stirring often, until the mixture is fairly thick, about 30 minutes. Set aside to cool.

FOR THE DOUGH: In a large heated bowl, combine the yeast, warm water, and $^1/_2$ teaspoon sugar, and stir until the yeast is dissolved. Set in a warm place for about 5 minutes until foamy. Combine the $^1/_2$ cup sugar, melted butter, and salt. Add the boiling water, stir, and cool until lukewarm (about 115°). Add to the yeast mixture. Stir in the beaten eggs. Add the flour gradually, turn out on a floured board, and knead about 5 minutes. The dough will be softer than bread dough. Place in a greased bowl, cover, and set in a warm place to rise until doubled in bulk.

Cover a work table with a piece of canvas or a cloth large enough to cover the entire table. Sprinkle flour lightly over all.

Put the dough in the center and roll out as thin as possible with a rolling pin, maintaining a square or rectangular shape. Then place the hands, palms up, under the dough and start stretching it in all directions, still maintaining the proper shape, until it is as thin as possible—as thin as a sheet of paper if you can manage this.

Spread the pulled dough evenly with the prepared filling. Sprinkle with cinnamon if desired. Roll up the patica as for a jelly roll by lifting up the cloth on one side and letting the dough roll itself up. Place in a large greased baking pan 2 inches deep, and form the pastry into an "S" shape. Tuck in the ends. Flatten it a little with the hands. Cover and let rise in a warm place for $2^{1}/_{2}$ hours.

Meanwhile, preheat the oven at 375°. Bake the patica for 10 minutes, reduce the oven heat to 350°, and bake about 50 minutes longer until it is nicely browned. Do not allow it to burn. Cool in the pan for 30 minutes. Remove and finish cooling on a wire rack.

MAKES 1 VERY LARGE PASTRY

MAKSALAALIKKO
(Finnish Rice and Liver Pudding)

    3 *tablespoons butter*
    1 *onion, chopped*
    $^{1}/_{2}$ *pound liver*
    $^{3}/_{4}$ *cup water*
    2 *cups rice*
    3 *cups milk*
    1 *cup water*
    $^{3}/_{4}$ *teaspoon salt*
    $^{1}/_{2}$ *cup raisins*
    3 *tablespoons molasses*
    $^{1}/_{4}$ *teaspoon pepper (or to taste)*
    $^{1}/_{4}$ *teaspoon marjoram*

Melt the butter and sauté the onions. Remove the onions and sauté the liver in the same pan for about 10 minutes. Add the

$^3/_4$ cup water and simmer 5 to 10 minutes, or until tender. Let cool. Chop the liver.

Meanwhile, cook the rice in the milk, the 1 cup water, and the salt until tender, about 20 minutes, stirring frequently with a fork. Preheat the oven at 350°. Mix together the sautéed onion, chopped liver and pan juices, and cooked rice, along with the raisins, molasses, pepper, and marjoram. Turn into a buttered 2$^1/_2$-quart baking dish and bake 20 minutes. Serve with melted butter.

MAKES 4 OR 5 SERVINGS

Festival Facts

The Duluth Folk Festival, which began in 1948, is held annually on the first Saturday in August at Leif Erikson Park, on the shore of Lake Superior in Duluth. Duluth, in northwestern Minnesota, can be reached from U.S. 2, 53, or 61, or Interstate 35. For further information, write: Duluth Folk Festival, 16 North Sixteenth Avenue, Duluth, Minnesota 55812.

Worthy of note is the big Festival of Nations, which is held every three years at the St. Paul Civic Center, St. Paul, Minnesota. For further information, write: International Institute of Minnesota, 1694 Como Avenue, St. Paul, Minnesota 55108.

14

New York, New York

Thousands of electric lights arched over the streets, shouts of players and promoters of games of chance, and the tempting aroma of green peppers and onions frying—all pinpoint from blocks and blocks away the Feast of San Gennaro, New York's most famous street fair.

The people who came from Naples to settle in the city's "Little Italy" a generation or more ago, and their many descendants who live there today, honor their patron saint, San Gennaro, or St. Januarius, each year in September with solemn Masses, religious processions, and the worldly enjoyment of games and Neapolitan goodies dispensed almost nonstop from dozens of food booths during the eleven days of the festival.

Gorging, rather than nibbling, seems appropriate in the fair's robust atmosphere, and one couldn't do better than to start with calzone. Calzone, which means "pants," is a deep-fried turnover made from pizza dough and stuffed with anything that comes into the mind of the cook who makes it. The San Gennaro version is filled with ham and ricotta and mozzarella cheeses.

The next course in this al fresco dining could be a sausage sandwich made with sweet Italian sausage charcoal-broiled and served hero-style on good Italian bread with fried onions and green peppers. Other booths offer sweetbread sausage, eggplant, stuffed artichokes, pizza, oysters, clams, and more. For those who'd rather sit, watch, and eat at table, there are any number of Italian restaurants along the festival streets that serve their own specialties.

Available in many booths—and a must for dessert—is zeppole, a sugar-dusted doughnut chewy in texture and gently spiced with mace. Ice creams, Italian ices, Italian pastries, candies, and espresso coffee are all available in abundance to fill any last bit of space the festival-goer might possibly have left.

Recipes for the fair's Calzone, Sausage Sandwich with Fried Peppers and Onions, and Zeppole follow.

CALZONE
(Ham and Cheese Turnovers)

> 1 *package active dry yeast*
> 1 *cup lukewarm water (about 115°)*
> 1 *teaspoon sugar*
> 1 *teaspoon salt*
> 1 *tablespoon liquid shortening or oil*
> $2^1/_2$ *to 3 cups flour*
> $^1/_4$ *pound mozzarella*
> $^1/_2$ *pound ricotta (if not available, use cottage cheese forced through a fine sieve)*
> 8 *thin slices prosciutto (if not available, use thin slices boiled ham)*
> *Cooking oil*

Place the yeast, water, and sugar in a large bowl and stir until the yeast is dissolved. Set in a warm place for about 5 minutes until foamy. Add the salt and liquid shortening or oil and mix well. Gradually add enough flour to make a dough barely firm enough to handle, mixing well. Knead on a lightly floured board until smooth. Divide the dough into 8 equal parts, shape into balls, and arrange on an oiled pan with high sides, allowing about 4 inches between balls. Flatten slightly. Cover the pan and allow the dough to rise in a warm place until doubled in bulk, about 1 hour.

While the dough is rising, coarsely grate or shred the mozzarella and combine in a bowl with the ricotta. If the mixture is very stiff, add a tablespoonful of milk. Cover and set aside.

When the dough has risen, place the dough balls on a floured board and flatten with the fingers, turning and shaping, until they are 6 or 7 inches in diameter. The balls may also be lifted and stretched in the air, but make certain not to create any very thin areas in the dough. Place a slice of prosciutto on each circle, and place one-eighth of the cheese mixture on each. Fold the prosciutto neatly around the cheese, making sure to encase it completely. Fold the dough over the filling in turnover fashion, or in a half-moon shape, and pinch the edges together well.

Heat the oil in a deep fryer until hot but not smoking. Lower the calzone, 1 or 2 at a time, into the oil and fry, turning, until nicely browned on both sides. Drain on paper towels. Serve hot. Calzone are eaten with the fingers, like pizza.

MAKES 8

SAUSAGE SANDWICH WITH FRIED PEPPERS AND ONIONS

$1^1/_2$ to $1^3/_4$ pounds sweet Italian sausage
$^1/_3$ cup olive oil
3 medium-sized onions, sliced
3 green peppers, cut into strips
1 garlic clove, crushed
$^1/_2$ teaspoon salt
$^1/_4$ teaspoon pepper
6 six-inch wedges Italian bread

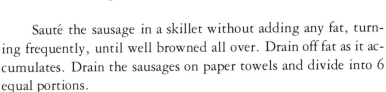

Sauté the sausage in a skillet without adding any fat, turning frequently, until well browned all over. Drain off fat as it accumulates. Drain the sausages on paper towels and divide into 6 equal portions.

Meanwhile, heat the olive oil in a skillet and add the onions, green peppers, garlic, salt, and pepper. Cook over moderate heat, stirring constantly, for 5 minutes. Lower the heat, cover, and continue cooking about 15 minutes, stirring occasionally, until the vegetables are soft but not mushy.

Slice through the bread wedges sandwich-fashion. Fill each wedge with a portion of sausage and some of the fried peppers and onions. Serve hot.

MAKES 6 SERVINGS

ZEPPOLE
(Neapolitan Doughnuts)

2 cups flour
$^1/_4$ teaspoon salt
3 teaspoons baking powder
$^1/_4$ teaspoon mace
2 eggs
$^1/_3$ cup sugar
$^1/_2$ cup milk
Vegetable oil
Confectioner's sugar

Have all ingredients at room temperature. Sift the flour, salt, baking powder, and mace into a bowl. Beat the eggs lightly, add the sugar, and continue beating until well blended. Stir in the milk. Pour into the flour mixture and mix well. Cover the bowl with plastic wrap and allow to sit at room temperature for 20 minutes.

Heat the vegetable oil in a deep fryer or wok to 370°, or until a 1-inch cube of bread browns in 1 minute. Slip the batter, which will be quite thick, by scant tablespoonsful into hot oil, making about 3 or 4 Zeppole at a time. Allow to fry about 3 minutes until golden—they will turn themselves over. Remove and drain on paper towels. Roll in, or sprinkle with, confectioner's sugar. May be eaten warm or cold.

MAKES ABOUT 24

Festival Facts

The Feast of San Gennaro is held for eleven days in mid-September and is centered at Broome and Mulberry Streets, which may be reached by subway, taking the Lexington Avenue local (not express) to Broome Street station in New York, New York. For further information, write: New York Convention and Visitors Bureau, Inc., 90 East Forty-second Street, New York, New York 10017.

Florida Folk Festival

15

White Springs, Florida

Spanish Bean Soup, Collard Greens with Cracklin' Corn Bread, Indian Fry Bread, Boiled and Parched Peanuts, Fried Catfish with Hush Puppies and Grits. Is there one place where this seemingly unrelated melange of foods can be found, and, if so, what's the reason for its diversity?

The foods can indeed all be found at Florida's Folk Festival, and their strange variety is due to the different cultures of the people who live in the state and delight in meeting to share their foods and folkways at the state's annual celebration. Right on the banks of the famous Suwannee River, immortalized long ago by Stephen Foster in "Old Folks at Home," both the old folks and the new with a mutual interest in their heritage gather to play their folk music, tell their folktales, do their own dances, demonstrate their special crafts, and share their distinctive foods. The Seminole Indians, Florida's first inhabitants, the descendants of the sixteenth-century Spanish, French, and English settlers, and West Indians, Italians, Hungarians, Greeks, Czechoslovakians, Cubans, and other "latecomers" are all represented, although some more pronouncedly than others.

One of the more outstanding groups represented, at least from a culinary point of view, is that of the Florida Crackers. It's a matter of debate what a Florida Cracker really is, and no one seems to know the origin of the term, but one theory is that the name came from the cracking sound of the whips used by the many drivers of ox teams that worked in Florida generations ago. The whips, making sounds like rifle shots when properly handled, announced that the "crackers" were coming. Today's Florida Crackers are fourth- and fifth-generation representatives of those early settlers whose life-styles, food preferences, and use of available ingredients melded to produce a cuisine distinctly Floridian. Some of their dishes are enjoyed in other parts of the South, but classified, nevertheless, as Florida Cracker cooking are things like chicken with dumplings (tough and chewy—not puffy—is the way they like them), black-eyed peas with onions and corn bread, hush puppies and fried catfish, grits and red-eye gravy, fried sweet potatoes, ham in biscuits, and hog head cheese. Not a cracker, you will note, is to be found in Cracker cooking.

A number of Cracker dishes are sold at the festival, among these Collard Greens with Cracklin' Corn Bread, the recipe for which has been provided by the festival's Jessie Mae Roberts of White Springs, Florida, and Fried Catfish with Hush Puppies and Grits Dinner, the recipe for which also appears through the kindness of festival participants. Because Florida was first settled by the Spanish, one expects to, and does, find influences of Spanish cooking in the area, and so it is not surprising that a succulent Spanish Bean Soup is one of the festival specialties. Ethel McDonald of Lake City, Florida, who is in charge of its preparation for the event, has donated her recipe, as shown below. Indian Fry Bread is another popular item, and is made by Richard

Clarke of Tampa, who learned the technique from several Seminole Indians. His recipe is given below. A much-loved local dessert is Pecan Pie, and the recipe for it has been donated by Lafayette McCall, who prepares it for the festival.

All the regional foods at the Florida Folk Festival are sold in a large food shelter and can then be toted to one of the many picnic tables on the grounds. If one is lucky, the music of one of the Carillon Concerts might come drifting by, for the music of Stephen Foster is unendingly popular at the Stephen Foster Center where the festival is held. Through the years, and right up to today, "Old Folks at Home" has been the most popular of Foster's works heard there, and visitors to the festival also like to hear "Kentucky Home," "Camptown Races," "Oh, Susanna," "Jeanie with the Light Brown Hair," and "Beautiful Dreamer," all written by the man considered to be one of our country's first-rate song composers, whose work had a profound influence on minstrel shows and other entertainment media of his day.

The story goes that one day when Stephen Foster was visiting some neighbors, their household servant, Nelly Bly, peeked into the parlor while the group was singing to the accompaniment of Stephen Foster at the piano. Foster asked what her name was, and upon hearing the reply, "Nelly Bly," struck up a tune in her honor. Nelly is now remembered not only in the song but in the name of a permanent restaurant, Nelly Bly's Kitchen, on the grounds of the Stephen Foster Center. One of the recipes below is for one of the house favorites, Brunswick Stew.

While certain groups, such as the Czechoslovakians and the Greeks, live too far from White Springs to be represented at the festival with their food specialties, most dishes being prepared in advance and carried in to the main food tent for sale, they compensate by presenting, instead, smartly costumed companies of dancers to take part in the festival's vast entertainment program. There's a Spanish Dance Company as well, some Irish Country Dancers, and a twosome that specialize in the sailor's hornpipe. Each day of the festival, in fact, a widely varied program is presented, with many types of dances that include centuries-old Maypole dancing, folk dancing, square dancing, and mountain dancing such as clogging that make the audience wish they could get up and join in. Clogging, to the uninitiated, is Appalachian

Mountain dancing to square dance calls, and features a buck-and-wing step danced to the accompaniment of a string band.

The musical feast continues with folk songs and ballads, fiddle tunes and strawbeating, mountain dulcimer solos and duets, harmonica harmonizers, yodeling, the whining of the musical saw, the playing of twelve-string classical guitar, gourd fiddle, or banjo, and on Sundays an abundance of gospel singing and spiritual music.

Even rags are made to sound entertaining when a local shoeshine artist and shoe repairman does his "Shoeshine Rag," and the Florida Cracker makes his whip talk, too, during his act. Other folks delight the audience with tall tales of the ways of the Old South, or with chats about Seminole lore, or how place-names in Florida came into being. There's a Medicine Wagon Show every day, complete with magic act and yarns galore, and daily mini-concerts in addition to the regular programs of entertainment both under the sun and beneath the stars.

Don't leave the Florida Folk Festival without visiting the Craftsmen at Work exhibit. One of the more unusual crafts is that of dulcimer making. While you may hear a mountain dulcimer during the entertainment, the craftsmen provide you with an opportunity to see the instrument at first hand, see how it's made, talk with its maker, and perhaps even end up buying one of your own. All mountain dulcimers are made by hand, and so no two are ever alike, as Leroy Lamey, a dulcimer craftsman from Jacksonville, Florida, points out. The shapes of the instruments are beautiful in themselves, with "pumpkinseed," a curvy "lady," and "teardrop" being three shapes that Mr. Lamey makes, and he is not above saying that dulcimers make handsome wall hangings—as indeed they do—for people who don't want to play but do want to own one.

Pecking birds, cloth dolls, and other folk toys are made by the various craftsmen, and there are demonstrations of Appalachian Mountain broom making, old-fashioned lye-soap making, palmetto crafts, and glassblowing. Seminole Indians display their crafts, and one can buy Suwannee River coral jewelry, needlework, plants, pickles, or jelly cake as the mood suggests. There's something for everyone, and as a duet of folksingers are fond of saying, "The only thing better than the Florida Folk Festival is more of it."

COLLARD GREENS WITH CRACKLIN' CORN BREAD

Collard Greens

1 or 2 ham hocks (or 1 ham butt)
Water
3 to 4 pounds collard greens
2 or 3 hot pepper pods
2 tablespoons bacon fat (or to taste)
$^1/_3$ teaspoon sugar
$^1/_2$ teaspoon salt

Parboil the ham hocks or ham butt 1 hour in water to cover in a large pot.

Meanwhile, wash the collard greens well in several changes of water. Remove any tough stems and discard. Cut the leaves very fine.

If necessary, add enough water to the pot to measure about $3^1/_2$ cups. Add the collard greens, pepper pods, bacon fat, sugar, and salt. Bring to a boil, lower heat, cover, and cook 1 hour, lifting the greens from the bottom to the top of pot once or twice during the cooking. Remove the lid, raise the heat, and allow the liquid to boil down until there is only about half an inch in the bottom of the pot.

MAKES 6 TO 8 SERVINGS

Cracklin' Corn Bread

$1^1/_3$ *cups flour*
$^1/_3$ *teaspoon salt*
$^1/_2$ *teaspoon baking powder*
$^1/_3$ *teaspoon sugar*
1 $^1/_2$ *cups cornmeal*
1 *cup milk*
1 *egg*
1 *cup cracklings, finely chopped**

Preheat the oven at 350°. Sift together the flour, salt, baking powder, and sugar, and combine with the cornmeal. Add the milk and eggs, and mix well. Add the cracklings and blend thoroughly. Turn into a greased 9-inch-square baking pan and bake 20 to 25 minutes or until browned.

MAKES 9 SERVINGS

FRIED CATFISH WITH HUSH PUPPIES AND GRITS DINNER

Fried Catfish

Catfish (allow 1 pound, uncleaned, per person)
Salt and pepper
Cornmeal
Oil or fat for frying

If possible, select catfish 6 to 8 inches long. Have the fish skinned, heads removed, and gutted. If you are doing this yourself, first cut off the heads, fins, and tails. Slit open the bottoms and gut the fish. Next, remove the skin by stripping it off with

---

*Cracklings can be made from any number of pork products. You can use bacon rinds, the crisp browned skin of roast pork or baked ham, fatback, or pork rinds. If using rinds or fatback, cut into small pieces before cooking in a heavy pan on top of the stove to render the fat. Pour off the fat as it is rendered until only browned, crisp cracklings remain. Crumble with the fingers, and if the cracklings are tough, soak them in water until softened before using in the corn bread. Bacon can be used to make cracklings but is a rather expensive ingredient to use in such an earthy dish.

the fingers, starting at the head end and stripping it down toward the tail. If necessary, use pliers to pull off the skin. Wash the fish well and pat dry with paper towels. If you are using large fish, cut into sections. Salt generously and pepper lightly. Roll in cornmeal and fry in hot oil or fat until golden and crisp, turning once.

Hush Puppies

> 1 *cup cornmeal*
> 2 *teaspoons baking powder*
> *1/2 teaspoon salt*
> *1/2 medium onion, finely chopped*
> 1 *egg, beaten*
> *1/4 cup water (approximately)*
> *Fat for frying*

Combine the cornmeal, baking powder, and salt. Add the onion, egg, and enough of the water to make a firm dough. Cover and set aside for 30 minutes or so. Shape into small finger-size rolls or small round balls. Heat the fat in a deep, heavy skillet, wok, or deep fryer until hot but not smoking. Fry the hush puppies until brown on both sides, turning once. Drain on paper towels.

MAKES ABOUT 15. THE RECIPE MAY BE DOUBLED.

Grits

> 5 *cups water*
> 1 *teaspoon salt*
> 1 *cup grits*
> 2 *or more tablespoons butter*

Bring the water to a boil in a heavy saucepan. Add the salt, and pour the grits in slowly, stirring constantly. When the mixture boils, reduce the heat, cover, and cook slowly for 25 minutes, stirring occasionally, until it thickens. Stir in the butter.

MAKES 6 SERVINGS

SPANISH BEAN SOUP

1 *twelve-ounce package dried garbanzos or chick-peas*
1 *tablespoon salt*
Water
Ham bone
6 *slices bacon, cut up*
1 *medium onion, chopped*
Pinch of saffron
Pinch of paprika
1 *tablespoon salt, or to taste*
1 *pound chorizos or smoked pork sausage, chopped*
1 *pound potatoes, peeled and diced*

Place the dried beans in a bowl with the salt and add cold water to cover well. Allow to soak 8 hours or overnight. Drain the beans and place them in a pot with 3 quarts of boiling water and the ham bone.

Sauté the bacon and onions together until lightly browned, then add them to the beans along with the saffron, paprika, and salt. Simmer 1 hour, covered. Add the sausage and potatoes and cook 1 hour more, or until all ingredients are tender. Remove the ham bone.

MAKES ABOUT 8 SERVINGS

INDIAN FRY BREAD

4 *cups self-rising all-purpose flour*
1¹/₂ *cups water (more or less)*
Lard for frying

Add the water to the flour, mixing well, for the mixture to have the consistency of biscuit dough. It should be dry enough not to stick to your fingers. Do not knead, as this tends to toughen the bread. Cover the bowl and set it aside for 1 or 2 hours.

Shape pieces of the dough into patties about 4 inches in diameter and ³/₈ to ¹/₂ inch thick. Melt the lard in a deep, heavy frying pan or wok to a depth of about 1¹/₂ inches. Heat until hot but not smoking. Test the temperature by dropping a small piece of the dough into the fat. It should sink, bubble, and then rise and float, still bubbling. Drop patties of dough 1 or 2 at a time into the hot fat and cook until golden-brown; then turn to cook the other side. They will puff as they cook. The first 1 or 2 will not cook too well, as they tend to season the fat. Drain on paper towels.

Serve plain or with white sugar, brown sugar, honey, or salt, or any combination of the four.

MAKES 10 TO 12

This recipe can be made with any amount of flour, adding water to make the dough the proper consistency.

PECAN PIE

¹/₄ cup butter
1 cup sugar
5 eggs, well beaten
1¹/₄ cups dark corn syrup
1 teaspoon vanilla extract
2 cups pecans
2 nine-inch unbaked pie shells

Preheat the oven at 300°. Cream together the butter and sugar. Add the eggs, corn syrup, and vanilla extract. Stir in the pecans. Pour into the unbaked pie shells, making certain the nuts are distributed evenly between the two shells. Bake 45 to 50 minutes. Cool on wire racks.

MAKES 2 NINE-INCH PIES

BRUNSWICK STEW FROM NELLYS BLY'S KITCHEN

2 to 2^{1}/$_{2}$ pounds chicken parts
1 tablespoon fat, oil, or drippings
3 cups boiling water
4 or 5 bay leaves
1 tablespoon salt (or to taste)
Pepper to taste
1 pound chopped beef
1 pound chopped pork
8 cups garden peas (if not available, substitute 1 two-pound bag frozen peas)
8 cups whole kernel corn (or 1 two-pound bag whole kernel frozen corn)
8 cups canned or fresh stewed tomatoes (3 twenty-eight-ounce cans)
6 cups peeled, diced potatoes

In a large, heavy pot, brown the chicken pieces in the fat, oil, or drippings. Cover, reduce heat, and cook until tender. Remove from the heat. Remove the chicken parts from the pot, and bone them. Return them to the pot, along with the boiling water, bay leaves, salt, pepper, beef, and pork, and combine thoroughly. Bring to a boil, lower the heat, and simmer for 10 minutes, stirring occasionally. Add the peas, corn, stewed tomatoes, and potatoes, and mix well. Bring to a boil, lower the heat, and cook about 1^{1}/$_{2}$ hours, or until mixture is quite thick, stirring frequently. Serve in soup plates. This stew is even better if prepared a day ahead and reheated.

MAKES ABOUT 16 SERVINGS

Festival Facts

The Florida Folk Festival, which began in 1953, is held annually for four days in September at the Stephen Foster Center on the banks of the Suwannee River, White Springs, Florida, which can be reached by exiting from Interstate 75 at Route 136, and travelling east three miles. For further information, write: Florida Department of State, Division of Cultural Affairs, Stephen Foster Center, P.O. Box 265, White Springs, Florida 32096.

Green Corn Dance

16

Onondaga Indian Reservation, near Nedrow, New York

Although the Green Corn Dance which is open to the public on the Onondaga Reservation is not considered the "real" Green Corn Dance by the Onondaga people, it's real enough to give one an opportunity to visit an Iroquois reservation, see Indian dancing, join in some fun and games, and taste some authentic Iroquoian food.

The Onondagas are one of the six nations of the Iroquois, and celebrate the "real" Green Corn Dance, a sacred ritual, in the privacy of their longhouse at the same time of year the public Green Corn Dance is held. Like other rituals, such as the Strawberry Ceremonial or the Green Bean Ceremonial, the Green Corn Dance is a festival of thanksgiving among the Iroquois. The work of planting and raising the corn has been finished and the crop assured, so the Indians feel it is time to give thanks for the corn and for harvest time, and they do this with certain dances, songs, games, and food which all have religious and spiritual significance. In days gone by, the Green Corn Dance was also a time for the coming together of scattered peoples for social activity prior to their separating again to head for their fall camps. The most important summer gathering for the Iroquois, the Green Corn Dance is a female, food-spirit-oriented one, as opposed to the Midwinter Ceremonial, the most lengthy and complex of the Iroquois ceremonials, and the most male-oriented.

Since soup is the basic food of the Iroquois, it is usually served in some form at festivals of thanksgiving. At the Strawberry Ceremonial, for example, soup containing strawberry juice is served, and at the Planting Ceremony, potato soup is made. It is not surprising, then, that corn soup is the main dish served at the Green Corn Dance. There are infinite versions of corn soup, varying from tribe to tribe and from cook to cook within a tribe, each making her own rendition, but basically the soup contains corn or white hominy, meat (usually pork in present times), beans, and vegetables such as squash or turnips.

Corn soup's typical accompaniment at the festival is ghost bread or scoons. Called "ghost bread" because of its use in ceremonies for the dead, it is also a little ghostlike in appearance, as it is very white and not given to browning when baked. It can be baked as a free-form loaf, put into a loaf pan, or changed into other shapes, using a different cooking method to become scoons. Scoons are made by rolling out the dough, cutting or breaking off pieces, putting a hole through the center of each piece, and frying in deep fat until brown. Corn bread is another specialty available at the festivities, as are corn on the cob, sassafras tea, and sometimes venison. The venison, when available, is usually served in the form of hamburgers, or venisonburgers, and is, of course, a recent, rather than old-time, Indian dish.

The Green Corn Dance to which the public is invited was started in the 1930s by Chief David Hill and is a fund-raising event for the First Volunteer Indian Fire Department of the Onondaga Reservation, a self-supporting group that receives no aid from any government source. It is held on the recreation field located in back of the firehouse on the reservation, and it is here that booths are set up, not only to serve food and drink (this being the only day of the year when beer is sold on the reservation) but to sell handcrafts and offer games of chance. While there are some ordinary souvenirs to be found, there are some treasures interspersed among them. There are beadwork items such as necklaces, earrings, rings, and pincushions, carved wooden pipes, headbands and watchbands, Iroquoian splint baskets and sweet grass baskets, soapstone carvings, and a small number of paintings by native American artists.

Among the games, the visitor can try his skill at archery or darts, and there are typical carnival-type attractions. If one is lucky, one might see—as at a recent festival—a peewee lacrosse game between teams of Onondaga boys. Lacrosse is an ancient sport played originally by many Eastern woodland Indian tribes that has been played with renewed interest in recent times.

Both men and women take part in the "social" dances of the Green Corn Dance, which are performed on the stage twice a day during the two-day event. Traditional Iroquois dancing attire is worn, and the dancers are accompanied by two or three singers who also play the water drum and rattles. One of the masters of ceremonies, who are authorities on the subject since each belongs to one of the Iroquois nations, explains the dances and their meaning before each performance so that one can have a proper feeling for the event and its importance.

The recipes that follow are for Ghost Bread and for Real Old-Time Iroquoian Green Corn Soup. Mrs. Louella Derrick of Nedrow, who has provided instructions for making the bread, says that it's made "by luck" and without measuring in Indian family cooking, but the measurements here turn out a nice crumbly baking-powder-biscuit-textured bread that Mrs. Derrick says should be allowed to cool a little after baking and then should be served with butter which melts deliciously into the still-warm bread. The Old-Time Corn Soup recipe is for those who want to try their luck and skill at building and cooking in and over an outdoor fire as the Iroquois did hundreds of years ago. This, incidentally, is the only untested recipe in the book, since I admit with regret to being the world's worst outdoor fire builder.

GHOST BREAD

4 cups flour
¹/₄ teaspoon salt
4 teaspoons baking powder
¹/₄ cup lard
1 cup skimmed milk (water or milk can be used, and skimmed milk
seems a good compromise)

Preheat the oven at 375°. Combine the flour, salt, and baking powder in a bowl. Cut in the lard with a pastry blender until the mixture resembles coarse meal. Add the liquid gradually, stirring constantly. Knead by hand when it becomes difficult to mix with a spoon. Shape into a loaf and pat down in a small loaf pan, about 4¹/₂x8¹/₂ inches in size. Bake about 35 minutes until the loaf sounds hollow when turned out of the baking pan and rapped on the bottom. Cool slightly on a wire rack. Slice and serve with butter.

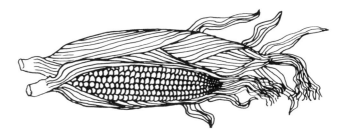

REAL OLD-TIME IROQUOIAN GREEN CORN SOUP

Remove the husks from green corn. Shell the corn from the cobs (remove the kernels) with the hands. Build an outdoor fire. When a good bed of coals is obtained, pack down the embers until they are level. Put the corn on top of the embers and stir with a stick, pulling the coals over the corn a little. When the corn has been cooked, pull away the ashes and fire. Place the corn in a coarse hominy basket or sieve and sift out the ashes and coals. Wash the corn in cold water. Place the corn in a kettle with water, and add meat, such as venison or pork, beans, such as kidney beans, and salt to taste. Boil until the meat is tender, stirring occasionally.

Festival Facts

The Green Corn Dance, which has been held as a public event since the 1930s, is held annually, generally on the third weekend in August, at the Onondaga Indian Reservation, Route 11A, Nedrow Exit, Route 81, near Nedrow, New York. For further information, write: Mrs. Louella Derrick, Indian Agent, Route 11A, Nedrow, New York 13120, or Greater Syracuse Chamber of Commerce, 100 Madison Street, Syracuse, New York 13202.

Prince Kuhio Festival

17

Kauai, Hawaii

The people of Hawaii's colorful islands pay homage to their equally colorful famous people each year with festivals, fun, and food that attract tourists and local people from miles around. The lilting names of the festive days are invitations in themselves: for instance, Aloha Week held all over the islands, the Merry Monarch Festival at Hilo, the Queen Liliuokalani Canoe Regatta from Honaunau to Kailua-Kona, and the Kamehameha Day Hoolaulea (picnic) at Honolulu honoring King Kamehameha the Great.

The island of Kauai is the scene of one such merry celebration each year in honor of Jonah Kuhio Kalanionaole, better known to his countrymen simply as Prince Kuhio. In legendary Hawaiian style, Prince Kuhio, the son of Kauai's last king, was born in a little grass shack on the flower-and-foliage-covered island late in the nineteenth century. Hawaiians revere him as their first and most charismatic delegate to the U.S. Congress, where he served ten devoted terms representing his people. On his festal day, they remember him with dances and songs of his own era, sporting and youth activities of this era, an elaborate royal ball, and, quite expectedly, a gigantic luau.

It isn't surprising that one of the traditional dishes of this and all Hawaiian luaus probably had its origins on Prince Kuhio's island. It was here that Captain Cook first set foot on the Hawaiian Islands, and in his wake came trading ships, whalers, missionaries, and, ultimately, settlers from many lands bringing strange new foods and introducing dishes that have had a lasting impact on Hawaii's cuisine. Not the least of these foods was salted salmon, which the Hawaiians at first abhorred but later came to enjoy so much that it's now the main ingredient of the indispensable luau dish, Lomi-Lomi Salmon. *Lomi* means "massaged," and the salt salmon is soaked, flaked, massaged with the fingers until smooth, combined with tomatoes and scallions, and served refreshingly chilled. It seems likely that Haupia, the coconut pudding that traditionally ends the luau, evolved from the cornstarch puddings introduced by early settlers from the mainland. Even the roast pig, a must at a luau, often finds itself being rubbed with ginger and soy sauce before being lowered into its baking pit, revealing the influence of Chinese cooking on the Hawaiian luau.

Luau means "taro leaf," one of the vegetables used extensively in preparing luau dishes. The word *luau* extended from the name of the leaf itself, to the dishes it appears in, and finally to the name of the feast at which these dishes are served. The main character at a luau is always kalua pig, which steams for many hours in its stone-heated ti-leaf-lined underground oven, along with sweet potatoes, bananas, and breadfruit. The taro plant appears again at the luau in the form of Poi, which is the root of the plant pounded into a paste. All the dishes mentioned here are served at all luaus, including the one at the Prince Kuhio Festival, along with other luau mainstays such as Chicken Luau, baked or broiled fish, pineapple spears, seaweed, small raw shellfish, and roasted kukui nuts.

Since underground oven cooking is as impractical for many Hawaiians as it is for most mainlanders, a smaller version of the luau, called a poi supper, has become very popular. It features a lesser number of luau dishes and substitutes a steamed pork dish, called Laulau, for the kalua pig. Authentic recipes or approved substitutes for all these dishes follow. Add some recorded Hawaiian music, flower leis for your guests, masses of green foliage and big paper flowers to decorate your dining room, and your mainland version of a Prince Kuhio Festival luau will be complete.

LAULAU

> 1 1/2 *pounds butterfish or mackerel*
> 3 *tablespoons kosher salt*
> 3 *pounds boneless pork*
> 72 *spinach leaves or taro leaves (or 36 Swiss chard leaves)*
> 24 *ti leaves* (or 48 cornhusks)*

Rub the fish with 1 tablespoon kosher salt and set aside. Cut the pork into 12 equal portions. Sprinkle with 2 tablespoons kosher salt and work in. Set aside.

Wash and remove the stems and fibrous parts from the spinach, taro, or Swiss chard leaves. Discard the stems. For each serving, arrange 6 spinach leaves or 3 Swiss chard leaves in a flat layer, all leaves facing in the same direction. Place 1 portion of pork on each serving. Cut the fish into 12 equal portions, and arrange over the pork.

Fold the leaves up at the bottom, over at the sides, and roll up as tightly as possible.

Prepare the ti leaves by partially cutting through the stiff rib and stripping it off. If using cornhusks, allow 4 wide husks

---

*Ti leaves are available at florist shops.

for each serving. One ear of corn will yield 8 to 12 husks. Place a fish-pork package at the end of a ti leaf and roll it up tightly, or use 2 cornhusks lengthwise, overlapped at the center, and roll them up tightly. Give bundles a quarter turn and lay them seam-side down on another ti leaf, or two more cornhusks, and roll them up into fist-sized bundles. Tie securely with string as if wrapping a package, tucking in any ends that may stick out. Place on a rack in a large pot containing 1 inch of boiling water. Cover, turn the heat to low, and steam $3^1/_2$ hours, checking the water level now and then. Remove with tongs, cut off strings, and serve. The cornhusks or ti leaves are not eaten.

If desired, Laulau can be made ahead, refrigerated, and steamed again 45 minutes before serving.

MAKES 12 SERVINGS

LOMI-LOMI SALMON

1 *one-pound slice of salmon*
2 *tablespoons kosher salt*
$^1/_2$ *cup lemon juice*
5 *tomatoes, peeled, seeded, and chopped*
1 *bunch scallions, finely sliced, including green tops*

Wash and dry the salmon and cut it into chunks. Rub with kosher salt and sprinkle with lemon juice. Place it in a glass or ceramic bowl and refrigerate, covered, 12 to 24 hours, turning occasionally.

Remove the bones and skin from the salmon. Shred and work the salmon meat with the fingers until it is smooth in texture. Add the tomatoes and scallions and mix well. Chill well before serving.

MAKES 6 TO 10 SERVINGS

POI

> 1 *can poi**
> *Sugar (optional)*

Heat the poi in a saucepan over a low flame. Cool before serving. Or follow the directions on the can. If the poi is too thick, it can be thinned with a little water. If desired, add a little sugar, which the Hawaiians recommend to first-time poi tasters. Eat with the fingers or with a fork.

MAKES 6 OR MORE SERVINGS

CHICKEN LUAU

> 1 *three- to three-and-a-half-pound chicken, cut into serving pieces*
> 1 *tablespoon butter*
> 1 *tablespoon oil*
> 1 *teaspoon salt*
> *Pepper to taste*
> $3/4$ *cup water*
> 1 *cup unsweetened, flaked coconut*
> $1^1/2$ *cups hot water*
> $1^1/2$ *pounds spinach*

Brown the chicken in the butter and oil, adding more butter and oil if necessary. Add the salt, pepper, and water, and cover the pan. Cook over low heat until tender.

Meanwhile, place the coconut and hot water in a bowl and allow to stand 30 minutes or longer. Then squeeze the coconut over and over with the hands. Drain in a sieve, pressing down with a spoon to remove as much liquid as possible from the coconut. Reserve the liquid, which is coconut milk, and discard the coconut.

Wash the spinach and cook in the water that clings to the leaves, until slightly wilted. Drain well. Put back in the pan and add 1 cup of the coconut milk. Simmer 2 minutes. Cut through

---

*Poi is available at specialty food stores.

the spinach with a sharp knife. Arrange the chicken pieces on a serving platter and arrange the spinach around it.

Heat the remaining coconut milk with the broth remaining in the pan in which the chicken was cooked. Pour over the chicken and spinach and serve.

MAKES 6 SERVINGS

PINEAPPLE SPEARS

1 fresh pineapple

Cut the pineapple into spears ¹/₂-inch thick, discarding the core and rind. If desired, canned unsweetened pineapple spears can be substituted for the fresh pineapple, although the results will not be as authentic. Arrange on a serving dish.

MAKES 10 OR MORE SERVINGS

BAKED SWEET POTATOES AND BAKED BANANAS

6 sweet potatoes or yams
6 bananas

Preheat the oven at 425°. Scrub and dry the sweet potatoes or yams and bake for 30 minutes. Pierce each potato with a fork and continue baking 15 to 30 minutes longer, or until potatoes can be pierced easily with a fork.

Put the bananas into the oven 15 minutes before the potatoes are done, without removing the banana skins.

MAKES 6 SERVINGS

HAUPIA*

2¹/₂ tablespoons cornstarch
3 tablespoons sugar
¹/₈ teaspoon salt
2 cups coconut milk†
Ti leaves (or magnolia or philodendron leaves)

Combine the cornstarch, sugar, and salt. Gradually add ¹/₂ cup of the coconut milk and set aside.

In a saucepan over low heat, cook 1¹/₂ cups of the coconut milk until hot. Add the cornstarch mixture, stirring, and cook, stirring constantly, until it is thick and the mixture coats a spoon. Pour into an 8-inch-square pan. Cool, cover, and refrigerate.

To serve, wash and dry the ti leaves well. Cut the ti leaves into squares, or use other leaves whole, removing the stems. Place a square of haupia on each leaf.

MAKES 9 OR 16 SERVINGS

Festival Facts

The Prince Kuhio Festival is held for one week around the time of Prince Kuhio's birthday, March 26, on the island of Kauai, Hawaii. The luau is held in Prince Kuhio Park, Kukuiula. For further information, write: Hawaii Visitors Bureau, 2270 Kalakaua Avenue, Honolulu, Hawaii 96815, or, in Hawaii, phone 808-923-1811.

---

*If you prefer, you may serve coconut cake in addition to, or in place of, haupia for dessert, as is sometimes done in Hawaii at poi suppers.

†Coconut milk can sometimes be bought in cans at specialty food stores, or you can make the proper quantity for this recipe by soaking 1 cup flaked unsweetened coconut in 2¹/₃ cups hot water for 30 minutes. Follow the balance of the procedure for making coconut milk in the Chicken Luau recipe (see page 125).

Holland Festival

18

Cedar Grove, Wisconsin

Swish go the street sweepers' brooms, clomp go the wooden shoes, and another annual Holland Festival is under way in Cedar Grove, Wisconsin. But before any of this begins, the burgemeester, chief official of the town in old Holland (and in this case the village president), and the town crier dress up in sixteenth-century Dutch clothing and drive all around town to proclaim to one and all that the festival has begun.

Out onto Main Street are wheeled ancient water-barrel carts to fill the buckets of the street scrubbers, who pitch into the Dutch rite of scrubbing the thoroughfare just as vigorously as people have similarly scrubbed their doorsteps, cobblestones, and pavements in Holland over the centuries. For the sheer satisfaction of keeping tradition alive, toddlers, teenagers, and people of all ages in ancestral Dutch garb swarm onto the street armed with brooms and brushes, buckets and pails—some swinging from shoulder yokes—to cleanse every inch of the way. A few spirited splashings and other watery tricks among fellow-scrubbers are part of the fun and add to the liveliness of the event, as does the final appraisal and approval of the scouring job by the inspekteur, a sort of Dutch counterpart of El Exigente.

Now the dancing begins on the spotless street, with accordianists, as of old, providing the music. Klompen are wooden shoes, so the dancers who perform wearing them are called klompen dancers, and their shoes beat rhythmically on the concrete in unison with the Dutch tunes. Charming to see and to hear, but not so easy on the feet, the shoes cause some of the dancers to wear as many as eight to ten pairs of socks for protection against the hard wood, and sometimes to reinforce that padding with sponges. No matter what is worn inside the shoes, though, the outermost pair of socks is always black. Most of the klompen dancers are girls, some of whom wear the costumes of boys, and all are proficient enough at their art to perform at various events throughout Wisconsin, and were the sole ethnic group to represent their state in Washington, D.C.'s big Bicentennial Parade in 1976.

Should one want to consider trying on or buying one's own pair of wooden shoes, for dancing or otherwise, a visit to the festival's klompenhouwer (wooden-shoe maker) is in order. Practicing the old-time craft with deft hands, he carves shoes from presoaked basswood or poplar using tools passed down to him through generations, and is happy to shape a pair in any size from the smallest child-size upward.

On to the Dutch treats, and two to have at the festival are worstebroodjes and oliebollen. Worstebroodjes consist of seasoned sausage meat baked in bread-dough jackets, and the aroma of their cooking floats tantalizingly in the air around the booth where they are sold. Oliebollen are holeless doughnuts, and are said to be the world's original doughnuts. They are made in a number of variations and are popular in Holland all year round as well as on Christmas Eve when they are served by the platterful. Another Dutch favorite is found at the erwtensoep stand.

Erwtensoep, Dutch pea soup, is savored by winter skaters on Holland's canals as much as it is by summer visitors at the Holland Festival.

A good selection of other ethnic specialties is available in many food booths, and should one want to have a sit-down dinner, it would not be amiss to visit the town's restaurants, which feature special Dutch dishes at festival time.

Many families appear at the festival in traditional Dutch costumes, but some of the nicest are those worn by the festival Queen and her Attendants. These sixteen- to nineteen-year-old girls all wear costumes representing different Dutch provinces. Copied from pictures of authentic regional Dutch clothing or authentically dressed Dutch dolls, the garments are stitched with care by local women who are proud of their Dutch heritage and enjoy making part of it visible for the festival-goer.

Make sure to see a korf ball game, which was recently introduced to this country by touring teams from Holland, and has since become a festival feature. Made up of teams that include both men and women, the game is somewhat similar to basketball.

Many other activities are planned to fill the Dutch day pleasantly, and these include an art fair on the green, Optocht units (a parade), a variety show which includes a barbershop quartet, a concert, a visit to the recently opened Het Museum (once a blacksmith's shop), which has begun to collect Dutch artifacts contributed or lent principally by the townspeople, and a number of bus tours. Throughout the day various groups of klompen dancers appear here and there around the festival to keep the atmosphere gay. At day's end, there is a Dutch Finale Dance where all can dance their cares away to the spirited Dutch music.

The recipes that follow are for the festival's raisin-studded Oliebollen and Cedar Grove's ham-laden Erwtensoep scaled down to family size.

OLIEBOLLEN
(Dutch Doughnuts)

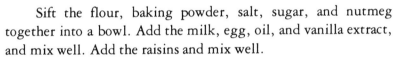

> 1¹/₂ *cups flour*
> 2 *teaspoons baking powder*
> ¹/₂ *teaspoon salt*
> 6 *tablespoons sugar*
> ¹/₄ *teaspoon nutmeg (optional)*
> ¹/₂ *cup milk*
> 1 *egg*
> 2 *tablespoons corn oil*
> ¹/₂ *teaspoon vanilla extract*
> ¹/₂ *cup raisins*
> *Oil for frying*
> *Sugar*

Sift the flour, baking powder, salt, sugar, and nutmeg together into a bowl. Add the milk, egg, oil, and vanilla extract, and mix well. Add the raisins and mix well.

Heat the oil in a deep-fat fryer or wok to 350° to 375°. Drop the batter by heaping teaspoonsful into the oil and brown on both sides, turning the balls that do not turn themselves over. Drain on paper towels. Roll in ordinary sugar.

MAKES 2¹/₂ DOZEN. THE RECIPE MAY BE DOUBLED.

ERWTENSOEP
(Dutch Pea Soup)

> ¹/₂ *ham with bone in (5 pounds or less)*
> *Cold water*
> 3 *cups split green peas*
> ¹/₃ *to* ¹/₂ *cup finely chopped onion*
> 1 *carrot, cut very fine*
> 1¹/₂ *stalks celery, cut very fine*
> *Salt to taste*

Place the ham in a large soup kettle and cover with cold water. Bring to a boil, remove any scum that rises to the surface, reduce the heat, and simmer $1^1/_2$ hours or until tender. Remove the ham from the water and add the split green peas, onion, carrot, and celery to the ham water in the pot. Add enough boiling water so that the contents of the pot measure between 3 and 4 quarts. Remove the ham from the bone and put the bone back in the soup pot.

Simmer the soup $1^1/_2$ hours, until the peas have fallen apart completely and the flavors are well blended, maintaining the same amount of liquid throughout the cooking time. While the soup is cooking, cut the ham into small pieces, and add it to the soup about 30 minutes before it has finished cooking. Add salt to taste. Remove and discard the ham bone.

MAKES 3 TO 4 QUARTS

Festival Facts

The Holland Festival, which began in 1947, is held annually on the last Friday and Saturday in July in Cedar Grove, Wisconsin, which is on Route 32, about ten miles south of Sheboygan Falls near Lake Michigan. For further information, write: Holland Festival, % Holland Guild Gezelschap, Cedar Grove, Wisconsin 53013.

Iowa State Fair

19

Des Moines, Iowa

As the editor of the *Fairfield Ledger* said when referring to the corn samples he had seen at Iowa's first state fair, "It is useless to talk of finding any better." That was back in 1854, and Iowans, continuing to prove in each passing era that their corn is without equal anywhere, bring along proof positive to their Corn Belt fair yearly to squelch any doubters. About ninety years after the birth of the Iowa State Fair, the principal event of that year's celebration, to corn growers at least, was the inception of the National Tall Corn Contest, which was won by an Iowan farmer who produced for inspection a twenty-three-foot, two-and-a-half-inch-high specimen of homegrown cornstalk. Today's farmers continue to produce "high-as-an-elephant's-eye" examples.

Displays by the hundreds, not only of corn but other vegetables, grains, fruits, meats, dairy products, flowers, landscaping plants, honeys, and wines, as examples of Iowa's diversified agriculture, are housed in the fair's turn-of-the-century Agricultural Building, a point of interest in itself as one of the best remaining examples of exposition-style architecture to be found anywhere in the world. Under its roof the best of Iowa's produce is judged and awarded blue ribbons as a tribute to the excellence of the land upon which it grows and the know-how of the people responsible for its growing.

Enjoying a national reputation as the best agricultural exposition in the country, the Iowa State Fair also has the most impressive livestock show in America. Here, for example, on the Avenue of Breeds in the Cattle Barn, one can see descendants of the first cattle brought to America by the Spanish. We call them longhorns, and they are only one of the many exotic breeds from foreign lands on display. In sheer number of head, the size of the livestock exhibits is staggering. If one were to count up all the animals shown by 4-H groups, farmers, and breeders, one would probably still be counting past fourteen thousand head of cattle, sheep, hogs, and horses which are presented for judging or entered in various contests. Besides that, there are scores of rabbits and various types of poultry to be seen, and a Grandfather's Farm to be visited.

The Iowa State Fair, which has had a number of "firsts" in its livestock features, was the first to require butchering of grand champion swine for meat-type hog evaluation, to have beef carcass shows and a lamb carcass evaluation, to weigh breeding beef cattle as they enter the show ring, and to hold attitude and appearance contests for swine exhibitors.

The purpose behind the breeding and growing of superior stock is, after all, the production of superior meat to grace the tables of America. In line with Iowa's interest in promoting its top-quality beef, pork, lamb, and other products, Barbecue Day was begun at the Iowa State Fair about fifteen years ago. At this outdoor meat-cooking competition, known as the Iowa Cookout King Contest, about a hundred winners from local cookout contests previously held all over the state merge to represent their communities in competing for first grand prizes in the Beef,

Pork, Lamb, Poultry, Turkey, and Novelty categories, as well as the Showmanship and Teenage categories. Succulent but simply prepared barbecued roasts as well as more imaginative and exotic meat dishes are prepared by the contestants.

The Showmanship Category allows the entrant to serve side dishes, have a table display, and be judged for suitable outdoor cookery apparel and neatness of cookout area, while the other categories stress excellence of meat preparation, wise use of a meat cut, and appetizing appearance of the finished product. Any male over the age of thirteen who is a resident of Iowa can enter the contest. When, if ever, the fair will feel inclined to sponsor both a King and a Queen Cookout Contest remains to be seen, but until that time, female entrants are confined to the age bracket of thirteen through high school graduation in the Teenage Competition.

Roger Candee of Fantanelle, Iowa, recently won second place in the Novelty Division of the Cookout King Contest for his Depression Dinner (recipe follows), which turns out to be not at all depressing, and, in fact, very delicious. It's a money-saving hamburger-stretching recipe that Mr. Candee worked out with the appetites of his three children—two of them always-hungry teenage sons—in mind.

Another winner, this one in the Beef Category, is Beef Supreme (recipe follows) entered by Richard Wonderlich of Mount Pleasant, Iowa. A truly sublime and very special-occasion dish, it has won other prizes for Mr. Wonderlich when he has made it with buffalo fillets in place of beef. Each year, too, the Wonderlichs make buffalo sandwiches, a rare treat indeed, at a local event in their town called Old Threshers Reunion. Mr. Wonderlich raises buffalo in addition to beef cattle and hogs, and at last count had fifty-two buffalo, whose meat he claims is juicier and requires less cooking time than beef. Moreover, buffalo don't eat as much as cattle and every part of a slaughtered animal can be utilized—as, for example, the buffalo head, which is in great demand for mounting for decorative purposes. Even the skeleton of one of Mr. Wonderlich's animals was sold for use in an exhibition.

Glazed Pork Chops (recipe follows) was a prizewinner for Mr. Marvin Anderson of Milford, Iowa, in the Pork Category. In the education profession for over eighteen years, Mr. Anderson knows a thing or two about cooking as well as schools. His specialty runs to cooking pork, and he's won prizes not only for his Glazed Pork Chops in more than one competition, but also for his Hawaiian Ham. While he, like most first-time entrants, felt a little nervous at his first Cookout King try, he's now an old hand at it and looks forward to future contests. The officials do such a good job of promoting a relaxed atmosphere, says Mr. Anderson, that you end up really enjoying the competition.

Foods for visitors to the Iowa State Fair run the gamut from carnival fare to South American and African dishes served in the International Place. Popcorn (made from Iowa corn, of course) ranks high as a booth-sold item, as do very popular corn dogs, which are hot dogs on a stick dipped in cornmeal batter and deep-fried. These novel franks originated during World War II when hot dog buns were in short supply because of the unavailability of wheat, and they have gained in popularity since that time. Thick-cut Iowa ham sandwiches, fresh pork sand-wiches, ham, bacon, egg and flapjack combos, fish and chips made in a special machine brought from London a few years ago and served in simulated British newspaper wrapping, prime steaks, economy loin cuts, fried chicken, candy floss (cotton candy), lemonade, root beer, and caramel apples are some of the items one can expect to find at the more than three hundred con-cessions scattered about the fairgrounds, each one of which is in-spected at least twice daily by the Department of Agriculture during the twelve-day run of the fair. The fair management itself also inspects and rates the concessions, thus maintaining clean, well-run, high-quality food operations on its grounds. One of the fair's recipes for Caramel Apples (in a home-sized version) is given below.

Back in the 1800s, people attending the fair more often than not arrived in covered wagons and camped on the grounds. In a sense, things haven't really changed that much, for today the fair still maintains a huge campground where people in vans and trailers, a little more in keeping with the times, stake out their claims for the run of the fair. Minibuses shuttle back and forth between the grounds and the "home-away-from-home" area to save wear and tear on the campers.

Horseracing, auto racing, top star entertainers, music, a ten-acre midway, a rodeo, and an Old Fiddlers Contest are some of the nonagricultural diversions offered.

The Heritage Fair, a permanent part of the grounds, has an Indian Village in which masterfully constructed wind- and weatherproof wickiups, once homes for the woodland Indians, have been made by Mesquakie Indians, and a seven-ton totem pole has been carved and erected there, too. The village also contains a replica of the Fort Madison blockhouse made from Iowa oak and partially surrounded by a section of stockade, and a sod house on Pioneer Hill is very much like those built by Iowa's original settlers who arrived in prairie schooners and built their homes from whatever they could utilize on the land.

While the theme of the fair in 1970 was "Discover Iowa" (for Iowans do love their state), they have since branched out to other, more far-reaching themes, including "Discover Mexico," to learn about the culture and customs of another land as well as to introduce Mexico to some of Iowa's products, "Discover Canada," to get to know their northern neighbors better, "Discover Hawaii," and just plain "The Discoverers," which honored Christopher Columbus, the land of his birth, and the land from which he sailed to America.

DEPRESSION DINNER

3 pounds ground round beef
2 medium potatoes, grated
4 large carrots, grated
1 large onion, grated
2 eggs
1 teaspoon minced garlic
1 tablespoon salt, or to taste
Pepper to taste
1/4 pound bacon, finely chopped*

Mix all ingredients together and form into about 14 thick
patties. Arrange on an outdoor grill over a medium fire and cook
10 minutes. Turn and cook about 5 minutes on the other side.

Patties may also be pan-broiled indoors for a similar length
of time with good results.

MAKES ABOUT 14

BEEF SUPREME

4 slices beef fillet, each cut 2 inches thick
4 tablespoons finely chopped onion
2 slices American or Cheddar cheese
Salt and pepper
1/4 cup red wine
2 tablespoons soy sauce
4 slices bacon
1 tablespoon water
1/2 teaspoon cornstarch
2 tablespoons butter
1 two-ounce can sliced mushrooms, drained

---

*If desired, each patty can be wrapped in a strip of bacon instead of chopping the bacon
and adding it to the mixture. In this case, you will need about 14 slices of bacon.

Cut a deep slit in the side of each fillet to make a pocket. Put 1 tablespoon chopped onion and $^1/_2$ slice cheese in each pocket. Sprinkle with salt and pepper. Close the pocket with a poultry pin or toothpick.

Combine the wine and soy sauce and brush the mixture all over the fillets. Broil them over hot coals about 25 minutes, or to your liking, turning them once during cooking and brushing them occasionally with the wine-and-soy sauce mixture. When half done, wrap a bacon slice around each fillet and secure with a poultry pin or toothpick.

In a small saucepan, combine the water and cornstarch. Add the butter, mushrooms, and wine-and-soy sauce mixture left over from basting. Stir until thickened, and spoon over the cooked fillets, from which the poultry pins or toothpicks have been removed.

MAKES 4 SERVINGS

GLAZED PORK CHOPS

8 pork chops, each cut about 1$^1/_2$ inches thick
4 ounces mint-flavored apple jelly
$^1/_4$ cup grenadine syrup
$^1/_4$ cup vinegar
$^1/_2$ teaspoon ground ginger
Salt and pepper to taste

Trim excess fat from the pork chops. Arrange on an outdoor grill, 4 inches from medium-hot coals. Turn after 15 minutes. Combine the jelly, syrup, vinegar, and ginger in a small saucepan and simmer about 5 minutes. Turn chops over and brush with the glaze. Continue to turn chops every 15 minutes, and brush each time with the glaze until a total cooking time of 1 to 1$^1/_4$ hours has been reached, or until meat has no pink left in the center. Season with salt and pepper.

MAKES 8 SERVINGS

CARAMEL APPLES

1³/4 *cups corn syrup*
2 *cups less* 2 *tablespoons sugar*
1 *fourteen-ounce can sweetened condensed milk*
3 *tablespoons coconut oil*
Pinch of salt
¹/4 *teaspoon vanilla extract*

Select hard, flavorful apples. Clean them and have them at room temperature. If freshly picked apples are used, they must sit for several days before being used for caramel apples. Insert a stick into each apple.

Place the corn syrup, sugar, condensed milk, and coconut oil in a saucepan or a large kettle. Cook, stirring, until the mixture reaches a temperature of 242°. Add the salt and vanilla extract, and mix. Turn off the heat.

Pick up the stick between the thumb and forefinger and insert the apple into the caramel so that the entire apple is covered, including the point where the stick enters it. Lift the apple just barely out of the coating and spin it to remove any excess coating, taking care not to splatter your hand with the hot mixture. As you raise the apple out of the saucepan or kettle, turn it with the bottom side up, so that the coating tends to run over the apple toward the stick. Set it, stick up, on a greased pan or foil and allow to cool.

MAKES ABOUT 1¹/2 DOZEN MEDIUM-SIZED APPLES

Festival Facts

The Iowa State Fair, which began in 1854, is held annually for twelve days in late August at the Fair Grounds, East Thirtieth and Grand Avenues in Des Moines. Des Moines is on Interstate 35 and 80 in central Iowa. For further information, write: Iowa State Fair Board, Fair Grounds, East Thirtieth and Grand Avenues, Des Moines, Iowa 50317.

Jambalaya Festival

20

Gonzales, Louisiana

The town of Gonzales, nestled in Louisiana's bayou country, boasts a two-hundred-year heritage of Creole cooking that has culminated not only in an annual festival honoring the most beloved of all Creole dishes, jambalaya, but in a declaration by the people of Gonzales that their town is undisputedly the Jambalaya Capital of the World.

There seems no cause to take issue with their right to the title when one considers the origin of their town. The first white inhabitants of the area were French-Canadian exiles who came in 1773, bringing with them an Acadian love for French cooking with its touches of garlic and herbs, and a willingness to adapt the subtleties of their seasonings to the foods locally available.

Within a few years Spanish settlers arrived, with leanings toward rice-based dishes like paella, enhanced by seafood, sausage, and chicken. From the melding of the culinary preferences of both these ethnic groups sprang the unique dish jambalaya, whose very name reflects its Spanish-French ancestry. It derives from the Spanish *jamon* and the French *jambon,* both meaning "ham," one of the principal ingredients of jambalaya, at least in its original form, and in some of its present-day variations as well.

Jambalaya was first served on a massive scale at the turn of the century, when church fairs were the major social events in Gonzales. The dish lent itself so well to quantity cooking that it soon became the traditional food served not only at family reunions, weddings, and similar celebrations, but also at every political rally and fair in the area.

Gonzales, which is named for Joseph Gonzales, the town's first postmaster, town planner, and, ultimately, mayor, held its first Jambalaya Festival in 1968, and they've been decking the town out every June since then for the big event. There's a parade where the year's Jambalaya Queen rides the Royal Float in full splendor, and there's music playing, dancing in the streets until all hours, rides for the kiddies, amateur boxing, one of the state's largest art shows, and last, but most importantly, the jambalaya itself.

Tons of jambalaya are dispensed to the festival visitors, who are seldom satisfied with one dish and are content only after two or three servings. For those obsessed with jambalaya gluttony there's the big Jambalaya Eating Contest, with the wiser folks cheering on their favorite gorgers from the sidelines.

The highest jambalaya honor is the title of World Champion Jambalaya Cook. The entrants in the contest for this title have spent years perfecting their own particular version of the specialty and start early in the day to cook, coax, tend, and stir with long wooden paddles their special pots of jambalaya. The cooking is done out-of-doors over hardwood fires, and the contestants give some of the credit for the special tangy flavor of their jambalaya to the oak- or hickory-wood smoke rising around their pots during the three hours of cooking. Honors are awarded by several judges who savor the contents of each pot with great care before making their decision.

Jambalaya cooking, whether done in competition or in any ordinary kitchen, has branched out into endless variations incorporating meat or seafood that includes chicken, sausage, ham, rabbit, pork, duck, squirrel, shrimp, or oysters, or combinations such as chicken-sausage, pork-sausage, chicken-pork, and shrimp-oyster. Probably the all-time favorites are shrimp or chicken, with or without ham, depending on the whim of the cook. The only real rule in making jambalaya is that it must be made with meat or seafood and with rice, in a ratio generally of two to one. For large gatherings that would mean 60 pounds of chicken and 30 pounds of rice, which would feed about 120 people.

Onions are always included in the Creole dish, as well as garlic and other seasonings, but while some cooks like to add tomatoes and green peppers, others (including most cooks in Gonzales) shun them completely.

The recipe for Shrimp Jambalaya that follows is one served at the Jambalaya Festival, and the recipe for Chicken Jambalaya is that of Mr. Uton Diez, a recent winner of the World's Champion Jambalaya Cooking Contest. A word of advice from the jambalaya experts of Gonzales—this is one dish you shouldn't rush. The slow browning of meat and onions is very important.

SHRIMP JAMBALAYA

2 *large onions, chopped*
2 *tablespoons oil*
1 *garlic clove, crushed*
1 *tablespoon chopped parsley*
1 *bay leaf*
Pinch of thyme
1$^1/_2$ *cups beef broth*
1 *pound shrimp, shelled, deveined, and washed*
1 *cup long-grain rice, washed*
Pepper to taste
Generous pinch cayenne pepper
$^1/_4$ *cup green-onion tops, chopped*

Slowly brown the onions in the oil. Add the garlic, parsley, bay leaf, and thyme, and stir for 1 minute. Add the beef broth, bring to a boil, and lower the heat. Add the shrimps, tossing lightly, and when the shrimps begin to turn pink, add the rice, pepper, cayenne, and green-onion tops. Cover and simmer until the rice is tender, tasting partway through the cooking time to see if more salt, pepper, or broth is needed.

Shrimp Jambalaya is nice with salad and corn bread. Leftovers can be used for stuffing green peppers.

MAKES 4 GENEROUS SERVINGS

CHICKEN JAMBALAYA

1 *five-pound fowl or hen*
1 *or* 2 *tablespoons oil*
3 *medium onions, chopped*
3 *garlic cloves, finely chopped*
7 *cups water*
3 *chicken bouillon cubes*
$2^1/2$ *pounds long-grain rice, washed*
$1/2$ *teaspoon pepper*
2 *tablespoons salt*
$1/2$ *teaspoon monosodium glutamate (optional)*
1 *tablespoon Worcestershire sauce*

Cut the fowl or hen into small pieces. Brown slowly on all sides in the oil. It will not be necessary to add more oil, as the fowl will release its own fat during browning. Remove the fowl and slowly brown the onion and garlic in the same pan. Put the fowl and onion mixture together in a large, heavy pot (cast iron is ideal) and add the water and chicken bouillon cubes. Stir gently. Cover and simmer 30 minutes or until the fowl is tender. Add the rice, pepper, salt, monosodium glutamate, and Worcestershire sauce, and stir gently. Cook over high heat, uncovered, until half the water has evaporated. Stir gently, lower the heat, cover, and simmer gently until the rice is done, about 30 minutes.

MAKES 10 SERVINGS

Festival Facts

The Jambalaya Festival, which began in 1968, is held annually on a weekend in mid-June in Gonzales, Louisiana, which
is on U.S. 61, about twenty miles south of Baton Rouge. For
further information, write: Jambalaya Festival, % Greater
Gonzales Chamber of Commerce, Gonzales, Louisiana 70737.

Kolacky Day

21

Montgomery, Minnesota

Will Rogers once sent word to Montgomery that he wished he could be present on Kolacky Day to eat a kolacky, although he had no idea how to pronounce it. That was back in 1932, and some people are still having a bit of trouble pronouncing it but no trouble at all in eating it. Thousands of people yearly swarm into Montgomery on Kolacky Day to down an average of twenty-seven to thirty thousand of the specialty, which is quite simply pronounced *ko-LAH-chee*. Montgomery, home to approximately twenty-four hundred people, is about forty-five miles south of the Minneapolis–St. Paul area, and is in Le Sueur County's corn- and pea-growing area, probably familiar to most people through association with the Jolly Green Giant, who has a canning and freezing plant in the town.

A kolacky, for those who have never been blessed with a sampling of the pastry, is a yeast-dough bun folded over a filling of prunes, apricots, dates, poppy seeds, or occasionally apples, and baked to a light golden brown. The prune filling is generally the most popular, so the buns available on Kolacky Day have prune for their filling. The name of the pastry derives from the word *kola,* which means "round" in Czechoslovakian, and the ending of the word defines a native sentimental attachment to the bun.

One might wonder why Montgomery, which is referred to familiarly as "Monty" by its inhabitants, should set aside an entire day presumably to sing the praises of a simple pastry. Kolacky Day is, in fact, a community event that dates back to a field day held in the fall of 1929 after local farmers had completed their harvesting and the season's crops had been processed at the local canneries.

Most of the farmers and workers were of Czechoslovakian descent, and since kolacky is a specialty of these people, nearly everyone, regardless of national background, felt that the Bohemian bun was a true symbol of their community as a whole. At the suggestion of the editors ("two of the staunchest Irishmen that Montgomery ever had") of the *Montgomery Messenger,* the town's still-flourishing newspaper, the community day was named Kolacky Day, with kolacky the pièce de résistance.

The first year's festivities included a free feed of corn, peas, kolacky, and coffee, but with the quick growth of the celebration in the following years, most of the gratis food plan had to be abandoned.

Most people who now attend Kolacky Day are content with eating a few of the pastry treats or buying a box of a dozen at one of the stands in various parts of town to take home for later nibbling, but those who can't resist kolacky's temptations with even a shred of restraint join in a Kolacky Eating Contest. The idea is to see how many kolacky each person can eat in a given period of time, and those whose digestive systems can withstand such a pastry onslaught manage to wolf down twenty or more of the buns in the allotted time. A glance at the winning names over the years shows that the champs come back to defend and/or fill themselves regularly at the contest, with the all-time record held by one Edward J. M. Barta, at latest count an eight-time winner, albeit in nonconsecutive years. Competition, while open to both men and women, seems to appeal more to the Montgomery male, since no woman has ever won the contest.

Kolacky Day is recognized as one of the oldest celebrations in the state, and its accompanying parade ranks as one of the largest and best in Minnesota. Features of some of the original old-time parades, such as the Doll Buggy Parade, the Twin and Triplet Marchers, and the King of St. Wenceslaus (patron saint of Czechoslovakia) Day float, have been replaced by the Queen and her Court along with other floats, antique automobiles, parade attractions such as bands, drum and bugle corps, drill teams, and clowns—in all, about 140 units of merriment.

Two days before Kolacky Day, always held on a Sunday, a Queen Pageant, with entertainment and the final selection of the Kolacky Queen, takes place at the local high school auditorium, and anyone wearing a Kolacky Button can gain entrance to the ceremonies. The yearly Kolacky Button, upon which the beautiful bun and the beautiful Kolacky Queen share equal space, has been sold since 1934 as a souvenir of the day.

A Kolacky Day Celebration Dance, also open to the public, follows the Queen Pageant at the American Legion Auditorium.

Kolacky Power, which is considered responsible for attracting the large crowds it does every year, has neither dwindled nor wavered through the years, although some of the old-time entertainment forms have gone the way of the ten-dollar gold piece. Kittenball (softball) games, tug-of-war competitions, free movies, airplane rides, and free watches dropped from airplanes to the crowds below have passed into Kolacky Day history. More contemporary—yet not necessarily more sophisticated—forms of celebration today are softball tournaments, polka bands, speeches by visiting dignitaries, and games of chance, all with sky-high mountains of kolacky forming the backdrop for the activity.

The following is the official Kolacky Day recipe for Bohemian Kolacky with prune filling. The recipe that follows it is for an alternate poppy-seed filling.

BOHEMIAN KOLACKY

FOR THE PASTRY:
  1 *cup milk*
  ¹/₂ cup butter
  1 *yeast cake or* 1 *package active dry yeast*
  1 *cup warm water (about 115°)*
  4 *eggs*
  ¹/₃ cup sugar
  5 *teaspoons salt*
  1 *teaspoon mace*
  6 *to* 7 *cups flour*

FOR THE FILLING:
  2 *cups prunes*
  2 *tablespoons melted butter*
  1 *tablespoon sugar (or to taste)*
  1 *teaspoon cinnamon*

FOR THE TOPPING:
  Melted shortening
  ¹/₄ teaspoon cinnamon
  2 *tablespoons sugar*
  Melted butter

FOR THE PASTRY: Scald the milk. Add the butter to the scalded milk and stir until dissolved. Cool. Add the yeast to the warm water and stir until dissolved. Set aside in a warm place for about 5 minutes until it starts to become foamy.

Beat the eggs and add the sugar, salt, and mace. Add the milk mixture. Add to the yeast. Add enough flour to make a soft dough, and mix well. Turn out on a floured board. Knead 10 to 15 minutes. Place in a greased bowl, cover, and set in a warm place to rise, about 1¹/₂ hours, or until doubled in bulk. (While the dough is rising, prepare the filling.) Punch down the dough and let it rise again until about doubled in bulk.

FOR THE FILLING: Cook the prunes in water according to package directions until well cooked. Drain, remove the pits, and chop fine. Add the melted butter and sugar. Add the cinnamon. If desired, chopped nuts may also be added. Set aside, covered, until the pastry is ready to be filled.

TO ASSEMBLE: Turn out the dough, half of it at a time, on a floured board, and pat to $^{1}/_{4}$-inch thickness. If necessary, use a rolling pin to get it thin enough. Cut into $2^{1}/_{2}$-inch squares. Place a spoonful of filling in the center of each square. Fold the opposite corners of the pastry together and pinch at the top, allowing the filling to show at the sides. Brush the tops with melted shortening. Arrange the kolacky on greased pans and let them rise in a warm place for about 30 minutes.

Preheat the oven at 325°. Mix together the cinnamon and the sugar, and sprinkle some lightly over each kolacky. Bake about 25 to 30 minutes or until lightly browned. Brush with melted butter.

MAKES ABOUT 6 DOZEN

Poppy-Seed Filling

$^{1}/_{2}$ pound ground poppy seeds
$^{3}/_{4}$ cup milk
$^{1}/_{2}$ cup sugar
3 tablespoons honey

In a saucepan combine the ground poppy seeds, milk, and sugar. Cook over low heat for 15 minutes, stirring constantly. Remove from the heat and add the honey. Cool. Cover. Set aside until the pastry is ready to be filled.

Festival Facts

Kolacky Day, which began in 1929, is held annually on a Sunday in mid-July in Montgomery, Minnesota. Montgomery is at the intersection of Routes 13 and 21, off U.S. 169 and Interstate 35, about forty miles south of the Minneapolis–St. Paul area. For further information, write: Kolacky Day, Montgomery Area Chamber of Commerce, Montgomery, Minnesota 56069.

22

Rockland, Maine

Nearly everyone who's ever tasted a Maine lobster has to admit they're the absolute best to be found anywhere in the world. The people in Rockland, Maine, set out to prove this point the first weekend of every August when they turn on the fires that heat up the water in their now-famous World's Largest Lobster Cooker and proceed to fill the stomachs of waiting lobster lovers, who come from far and wide, with some of their succulent Down East seafood. The lobster cooker, originated by one Captain Ote Lewis of Ash Point, Maine, is made from a tremendous oil barrel that holds seventy-five gallons of water and can cook five hundred lobsters at a time. Many loyal visitors have made attendance at the festival a tradition, referring to it as "the big lobster feed down in Rockland," and wouldn't miss it for anything in the world.

Even before the big lobster boiler gets to work on the first day of the festival, other ocean treats are readied to feast upon. Delicate Maine shrimps, a tiny sweet variety found in the cold coastal waters of the state, are fried golden-brown and eaten as prelobster snacks by some or added to lobster dinners by others.

A distinctive festival specialty is clam puffs, chopped Maine clams in a batter that puffs up into crunchy goodness upon being cooked. Sold in pint- and quart-size containers, clam puffs can be eaten alone or, like the shrimp, added to a lobster dinner. Steamed clams, fish portions, and other seafood is available, too, as well as blueberry pie, another Maine specialty, and various other foods and drinks, including an open-air pancake breakfast served as early as seven in the morning.

There's ample space to sit down and enjoy your lobster in the eating tent before heading out to tour one or more of the visiting ships standing in the harbor for the festival. Each year different ships come calling, so that one might see a Navy destroyer, Coast Guard minesweeper, or Coast Guard cutter, and free boat rides are provided to and from these ships. Nearly everything at the Seafoods Festival, in fact—with the understandable exception of the foods—is free, and nearly everything carries out the nautical theme of the festival.

If you haven't seen a lobster trap before, you'll want to visit the Maine Fisheries Tent, filled with marine exhibits and demonstrations by Maine fisherfolk who show such things as how to build a lobster trap, how bait bags are knitted and what kinds of twine and rope are used, what a lobster boat looks like, and how the fishermen go about the business of catching lobsters and other seafood. One couldn't ask for a more authoritative setting for learning about the workings of the fishing business, for Rockland is the state's leading port in fish landings. Here fish and shellfish are assembled and shipped out, sardines canned, and all the other work done that is necessary to keep the area's four-hundred-year-old history of profitable fishing alive.

Outdoors in the tangy salt air there's a marine parade featuring a fifty-five-foot-long lobster—hopefully a reproduction of the real thing—and a pageant featuring King Neptune, who presumably emerges annually from the briny deep to guide the merrymaking with his Royal Court of the Sea. The pageant and all other events are centered about Rockland's harbor and are within easy walking distance of each other. Noteworthy nautical places to visit are the Rockland Station Marine Exhibit, containing over a thousand artifacts of the Coast Guard, Lighthouse Service, and Lifesaving Service, and the William A. Farnsworth Library and Arts Museum, which has a fine display of ship models and articles used in the fishing trade, as well as a large collection of Wyeth family paintings.

Following are a recipe for Clam Puffs (provided by the Rockland Jaycees, who make them for the festival), the festival's at-home instructions for Boiled Maine Lobsters, and a recipe for the festival's Maine Fresh Blueberry Pie.

CLAM PUFFS

1 *egg*
1 *cup milk*
1 *tablespoon melted butter*
1$^1/_2$ *cups flour*
1 *tablespoon baking powder*
$^1/_2$ *teaspoon salt*
1 *pint fresh shucked clams (or canned minced clams, drained, if*
   fresh are not available)
Fat or oil for frying

Beat the egg and add the milk and melted butter. Sift together the flour, baking powder, and salt, and add to the egg mixture. Squeeze out the black area from the clams and grind the clams. Mix with the batter.

Heat the fat or oil in a deep fryer or wok until hot but not smoking. Drop the batter by tablespoonsful into the hot fat. Fry until brown, turn, and brown the other side. Drain on paper towels.

MAKES ABOUT 3 DOZEN

BOILED MAINE LOBSTERS

1 *lobster per person, weighing* 1 *to* 1^1/$_4$ *pounds each (or larger if desired)*
Boiling water
1 *tablespoon salt*
Melted butter

Place the live lobsters in a large kettle containing about 3 inches of briskly boiling salted water. Cover immediately. Bring the water to a boil again, and begin timing, allowing 18 to 20 minutes for cooking. Serve the lobsters whole, with a side dish of melted butter. Supply large table napkins to each person, as well as nut crackers or lobster crackers to break open the shells.

MAINE FRESH BLUEBERRY PIE

1 *cup sugar*
2 *tablespoons flour (or* 1^1/$_2$ *tablespoons quick-cooking tapioca)*
^{1}/$_8$ *teaspoon salt*
^{1}/$_2$ *teaspoon cinnamon (optional)*
Pastry for 2-crust pie
1 *quart fresh blueberries*
2 *teaspoons lemon juice*
1 *tablespoon butter*

Preheat the oven at 425°. Combine the sugar, flour or tapioca, salt, and cinnamon. Line a 9-inch pie pan with pastry and arrange half the blueberries in it. Sprinkle with half the sugar mixture. Repeat. Sprinkle with the lemon juice. Dot with the butter. Place the top crust over and seal the edges. Slash the top. Bake until the crust is nicely browned and the filling is bubbly, about 30 to 35 minutes. If the pie starts to brown too much, reduce the oven temperature to 350°.

MAKES 1 NINE-INCH PIE

Festival Facts

The Maine Seafoods Festival, which began in 1947, is held annually for four days in early August, centered around the harbor in Rockland, Maine, which is on U.S. 1. For further information, write: Rockland Area Chamber of Commerce, P.O. Box 508, Rockland, Maine 04841.

Maple Festival

23

Jefferson, New York

Long ago in early March, when the redwing blackbirds returned to the North, the Indians would begin to tap their maple trees to collect "sweet water" and to set up camps for maple sugaring. They called March "maple sugar month," devoted that time to preparing maple syrup and sugar to last them through the following year, and celebrated their good fortune with maple sugar ceremonies of thanksgiving.

As the Indians once started their sap-gathering at the time of a March full moon, so do we today begin the business of collecting sap in maple sugar country at the sign of the first spring thaw, and celebrate the marvels of maple in our own way with maple festivals in the major maple-producing states of America.

Among the colorful festivals, usually held in late April after the sap has stopped flowing and the arduous maple-sugaring work has been finished for the season, is the Maple Festival in Jefferson, New York. This festival represents the entire county of Schoharie, one of the state's maple-producing counties, and is a joint effort of the many maple-sugar producers and maple-sugar lovers of the area. Rumor to the contrary, New York State, not Vermont, is the largest producer of maple syrup in the United States, and Schoharians are proud of their more than two-hundred-year history of producing quality maple products. A visit to their Maple Festival gives the maple tyro a sampling of the wondrous tastes of maple, a feeling of the romance and nostalgia of sugarbush country, and a firsthand view of the actual steps in producing maple products.

Early arrivals at the festival can fortify themselves with a hearty breakfast of sausages and pancakes bathed in pure maple syrup, and go on to spend the balance of the day observing and tasting the many forms of maple. On the village green, tree tappers demonstrate the first step in maple making by tapping maple trees growing in the center of the festival's activities. Fragrant steam rises from a model saphouse where one can see how the sap evaporates and produces maple syrup, and can savor a sample of warm syrup the moment it comes out through the filter.

Fun to see and eat are eggs boiled in old-fashioned kettles full of maple sap, just as they were cooked long ago, before modern machinery replaced the kettle, to provide quick hot lunches for maple gatherers out in the deep woods. Even though the hard-cooked eggs pick up almost no flavor from the maple sap, they're nice to eat straight out of the shell in the out-of-doors.

A favorite with children at the festival is jackwax, or lockjaw, which is best described as a sort of edible maple chewing gum. To make jackwax, boiling maple syrup is poured in streams over crushed ice or freshly fallen snow, where it quickly cools and hardens into a sticky, chewy treat eaten by winding it around wooden forks like spaghetti.

Visitors intent on nibbling maple treats throughout the day can also have some stir-it-yourself maple sugar or a cup of coffee with some maple-sugar-coated doughnuts made by the women's auxiliary of the town's fire department. Maple cream, maple candies, and other maple products are for sale to take home.

For those who want to immerse themselves in maple lore, some years there is a display of antique maple-sugaring artifacts at a Maple Museum on the green, and there are sugar camps and farms nearby that welcome visitors to their sugarhouses all year round.

Before settling down to a maple-baked ham dinner at day's end, festival-goers can watch the Maple Queen Parade, see a lumberjacks' contest (hopefully cutting up trees other than maples), take a horse-and-wagon ride, or rest their feet while taking in some entertainment on the village green. In the evening there's country dancing, and for those in the know, a maple passion drink can be mixed up later at home to end an all-out maple day. The recipes that follow have very kindly been provided by Martha Dayton of Taylor Farms Sugar Camp, who takes an active part in the festival annually. Recipes include Jackwax, Maple Baked Ham, and Maple Frosted Cake as served at the festival, and Maple Passion Drink.

JACKWAX

Crushed ice or clean snow
1 cup maple syrup
Sour pickles (optional)

Fill 6 to 8 paper cups, small paper plates, or china saucers with crushed ice or clean snow. In a saucepan bring the maple syrup to a boil. Continue cooking until the syrup reaches 232° to 234°, or until a drop of syrup forms a soft ball when dropped into cold water. To hasten the temperature rise, cover the saucepan during cooking. Pour syrup in a thin stream over the ice in a circular fashion. To eat, pick up the jackwax by twisting it around a fork.

For an authentic touch, serve with sour pickles.

MAKES 6 TO 8 SERVINGS

MAPLE BAKED HAM

1 whole or ¹/₂ a smoked (cured) ready-to-eat ham
Whole cloves
1 cup maple syrup

Preheat the oven at 325°. Trim off any rind from the ham. Score the fat by crisscrossing with a knife to make a diamond pattern, and stud with the cloves, 1 in each diamond. Brush all over with the maple syrup, and set on a rack in a baking pan. Place in the oven and bake uncovered, allowing 10 minutes per pound, basting every 10 minutes with about ¹/₄ cup of the maple syrup until you have used up the 1 cup. Continue basting with the pan drippings every 10 minutes until the ham is done.

MAPLE FROSTED CAKE

FOR THE CAKE:
1 cup butter or margarine
2 cups sugar
4 eggs, beaten
1³/₄ cups sifted cake flour
3 teaspoons baking powder
¹/₂ teaspoon salt
1 cup milk
2 teaspoons vanilla extract

FOR THE FROSTING:
³/₄ cup maple syrup
¹/₄ cup water
¹/₄ cup sugar
1 egg white
Generous pinch of salt

FOR THE CAKE: Preheat the oven at 350°. Cream the butter or margarine and add the sugar gradually, blending well. Add the eggs and mix well. Sift together the cake flour, baking powder, and salt, and add to the batter alternately with the milk and vanilla extract. Pour into a greased 8x12-inch baking pan and bake 45 to 50 minutes, or until a cake tester inserted in the center comes out clean. Remove from the pan and cool on a wire rack.

FOR THE FROSTING: Combine the maple syrup, water, and sugar in a saucepan and bring to a boil. Continue boiling to 360°, or until the mixture spins a thread when stirred and lifted with a spoon. Remove from the heat. Beat the egg white well, and add the salt. Pour the maple mixture over the egg white, and beat just until it is thick enough to spread. Spread over the cake and cut into squares.

MAKES 12 SERVINGS

MAPLE PASSION DRINK

2 *tablespoons lemon juice*
$^1/_4$ *cup maple syrup*
6 *tablespoons whiskey*
Ice

Stir the lemon juice, maple syrup, and whiskey together with the ice. Pour over ice into 2 cocktail glasses.

MAKES 2 DRINKS

Festival Facts
The Schoharie County Maple Festival, which began in 1966, is held annually on a weekend in late April on the village green in Jefferson, New York. To reach Jefferson, take the New York State Thruway (Interstate 87) to Exit 21, go west on Route 23 to Stamford, and north on Route 10 to Jefferson. For more information, write: Maple Festival, P.O. Box 24, Jefferson, New York 12093.

24

Dothan, Alabama

Nuts to the crowds, thrown gracefully by feminine float riders and goofily by gawdy clowns, are part of the joyous parade that climaxes the week-long National Peanut Festival each year in Dothan, Alabama. The reason for the gaiety of both paraders and peanut-catchers is gratitude for the current year's crop of peanuts raised in the southeastern part of the state where the festival is held. Peanuts are the number-one agricultural crop of Alabama's "wiregrass country" and have been recognized as a vital part of the area's life since 1938, when the first peanut harvest time festival took place in Dothan.

Records from the early Peanut Festival days tell us that Dr.

George Washington Carver, one of America's most famous botanists, was a guest at the first annual gathering. Throughout the course of his life Dr. Carver did an astounding amount of research on the peanut. He found more than 105 ways it could be utilized as human food—among these, as a cooking oil, in beverages, punches, and the still-popular peanut brittle. Nor did he forget the needs of livestock when he developed feed for chickens, hogs, and other animals.

Dr. Carver would no doubt be pleased at today's festivals to see Mr. Peanut Farmer of the Year rewarded for raising the highest poundage of peanuts per acre on his land. Recently Peter Riley, a Covington County farmer, harvested over four thousand pounds per acre on his eighty-acre peanut farm to walk off with the festival's impressive Peanut Farmer of the Year award, an immense peanut-in-the-shell-shaped trophy standing several feet high. Although there are nine distinct varieties of peanuts grown in the United States, most Alabama farmers like Mr. Riley specialize in raising either Spanish or runner peanuts.

Whatever can one do with so many peanuts? One of the festival's main contests gives local cooks a chance to show what can be done with *some* of them. One of the most popular contests, held on the second day of the fair's activities, is the National Peanut Festival Recipe Contest, which stresses the nut as a healthful and nutritious ingredient to include in the diet. Here contestants tote in pies, cakes, candies, cookies, vegetable dishes, main dishes, and other edibles that feature peanuts or products of peanuts (such as peanut flour, peanut oil, or peanut butter). Recipes for the goods they bring for judging have to be submitted in writing two weeks before fair time. Three cash prizes are awarded in each of five categories of the contest open to both adult and teenage contestants.

An entry in one year's contest was Mrs. Leon Redding's grand-prize-winning Harvest Nutty Fruit Pie. The recipe for this open-top pie and other recent prizewinning recipes are included below. Since peanuts lend themselves so well to candy making, two of the confections are very attractive and good—Buckeyes and, quite expectedly, genuine Dixie Peanut Brittle. In the cake category there's Winkie's Peanut Brittle Yam Cake and a rich Peanut Butter Fudge Cake. For those who prefer their goobers in the main part of their meal, there's a Peanut Cauliflower Wiener Casserole.

Although almost unknown outside the South, boiled peanuts have a devoted following and a place all their own in the Canning Section of the Arts and Crafts Division of the festival. A boiled peanut is simply a peanut boiled in salted water in the shell, in which it is kept until ready to be opened and eaten like any other peanut. But it has a flavor and texture quite apart from that of a roasted peanut. Prizes awarded in the Canned Boiled Peanut and the Homemade Peanut Butter categories are based on both the quality and the appearance of these products, since little can be done to alter the ingredients used in their preparation. A Prizewinning Peanut Butter recipe by Mrs. Glenwood Hodges, who enjoys making up new ways to use peanuts in her cooking all the time, is given below. Both parched peanuts and boiled peanuts are prepared and sold by 4-H clubs and civic groups all during the festival.

No longer able to confine itself to its original weekend time slot, the National Peanut Festival has added events year by year until it now takes a full week to include all its goings-on. For those who like sloppy sorts of fun, one couldn't do better than take in the greased-pig contest. There are hog and cattle shows of all kinds, and a special calf scramble for young boys.

A Miss National Peanut Festival Contest is held among beauties from southeastern Alabama. The winning young lady is crowned Queen of the festival, reigns over it and its parade, and thereafter spends a good deal of time traveling about to promote the festival, peanuts, Dothan, the wiregrass, and the state of Alabama. "Keep pushing those goobers," they tell her, and push them she does, pinning tiny golden peanuts on as many lapels of as many honored guests at as many functions as time and decorum allow.

A Little Miss Peanut Pageant selects a junior version of peanut royalty, and there are youth and homemaking exhibits, soapbox derbies, bowling and golf tournaments, rock and country music shows, special guests, and a mélange of midway attractions, not the least of which include a man who dives forty feet into seventeen inches of water, a Hindu fakir complete with bed of nails, and a very fuzzy "almost-human gorilla."

HARVEST NUTTY FRUIT PIE

1 *nine-inch unbaked pie shell (or half of an 11-ounce package piecrust mix, plus 2 teaspoons peanut oil and 2 tablespoons cold water)*
$^1/_2$ *cup butter or margarine*
1 *cup sugar*
$^1/_2$ *cup flaked coconut*
$^1/_2$ *cup raisins*
$^1/_2$ *cup chopped peanuts*
2 *eggs, well beaten*
2 *teaspoons vinegar*
$^1/_4$ *teaspoon cloves*
$^1/_4$ *teaspoon cinnamon*

Roll out the pastry and line a 9-inch pie pan, fluting the pastry edges. (If using a piecrust mix, prepare it according to the package directions, using 2 teaspoons peanut oil and 2 tablespoons water.)

Preheat the oven at 350°. In a saucepan, melt the butter or margarine. Stir in the sugar, coconut, raisins, peanuts, eggs, vinegar, cloves, and cinnamon. Pour into the lined pie pan. Bake 30 minutes until brown and slightly puffed. May be served warm or cold, with or without whipped cream or vanilla ice cream.

MAKES 1 NINE-INCH PIE

BUCKEYES

$^1/_2$ *cup butter*
$^1/_2$ *cup smooth peanut butter*
$^1/_2$ *pound confectioner's sugar, sifted*
3 *ounces semisweet chocolate*
$^1/_8$ *block ($^1/_2$ ounce) paraffin*

Cream the butter until soft. Add the peanut butter, and cream until well blended. Add the confectioner's sugar gradually and mix well. Roll into balls about 1 inch in diameter, the size of buckeyes (horse chestnuts). Set on a plate and chill in the refrigerator 30 minutes or more. Melt the chocolate and paraffin in the top of a double boiler over hot water, stirring until smooth and well blended. Remove from heat. Using a wooden toothpick, dip each ball into the chocolate mixture, leaving the top un-coated for the "buckeye" effect. Set on aluminum foil. Re-frigerate until firm.

MAKES ABOUT 3 DOZEN. THE RECIPE CAN BE DOUBLED OR QUADRUPLED.

DIXIE PEANUT BRITTLE

2 *cups sugar*
$^1/_2$ *cup white corn syrup*
$^1/_2$ *cup water*
$1^1/_2$ *cups shelled roasted or raw peanuts*
2 *tablespoons butter*
1 *teaspoon salt*
1 *teaspoon baking soda*

Butter a sheet of aluminum foil about 2 feet long. In a heavy saucepan, combine the sugar, corn syrup, and water. Bring to a boil and cook to about 280° (soft-crack stage). Add the peanuts and continue cooking until the mixture is lightly browned. Do not overcook. Remove from heat and add the butter, salt, and baking soda. Pour onto the prepared aluminum foil immediately, making sure the peanuts are distributed evenly over the surface. Cool. Break into pieces.

MAKES 1 BATCH

WINKIE'S PEANUT BRITTLE YAM CAKE

FOR THE CAKE:

1¹/₂ cups peanut oil

2 cups sugar

4 eggs

2¹/₂ cups self-rising all-purpose flour

1 teaspoon cinnamon

1 teaspoon nutmeg

¹/₂ teaspoon allspice

1 cup grated raw sweet potato or yam

1¹/₂ teaspoons vanilla extract

FOR THE TOPPING:

2 cups crushed peanut brittle

1 nine-ounce container frozen whipped nondairy topping, thawed

2 teaspoons vanilla extract

FOR THE CAKE: Preheat the oven at 350°. Place all ingredients in the large bowl of an electric mixer, and combine. Beat 3 minutes at medium speed. Divide into 3 greased and floured 9-inch round cake pans. Bake 25 minutes, or until a cake tester inserted in the center comes out clean. Cool on a wire rack.

FOR THE TOPPING: Combine all ingredients and spread on the cooled cake layers. Sprinkle with additional crushed peanut brittle if desired.

MAKES 1 CAKE

PEANUT BUTTER FUDGE CAKE

FOR THE CAKE:

³/₄ cup butter or margarine

1 cup peanut butter (smooth or crunchy)

2¹/₄ cups sugar

1¹/₂ teaspoons vanilla extract

3 eggs

3 one-ounce squares unsweetened chocolate, melted

3 cups sifted cake flour
1¹/₂ teaspoons baking soda
³/₄ teaspoon salt
1¹/₂ cups ice water

FOR THE FROSTING:

¹/₂ cup peanut butter (smooth)
1 cup light cream
2 cups sugar
2 one-ounce squares unsweetened chocolate

FOR THE CAKE: Preheat the oven at 350°. Cream the butter or margarine until soft. Add the peanut butter, and cream until smooth. Add the sugar and vanilla extract. Add the eggs and beat until fluffy. Add the melted chocolate and blend well. Sift together the cake flour, baking soda, and salt, and add alternately with the ice water. Turn into a well-greased and floured 10-inch tube pan or three 8-inch layer-cake pans. Bake a large cake about 1 hour and small cakes about 30 to 35 minutes, or until a cake tester inserted in the center comes out clean. Turn out onto a wire rack. Cool completely before making the frosting.

FOR THE FROSTING: Place the peanut butter in a heavy saucepan and add the cream gradually, blending until smooth. Add the sugar and mix well. Add the chocolate and place the pan over a medium flame. Bring to a boil, stirring, and boil 3 minutes without stirring. Reduce heat and cook, stirring occasionally, to the soft-ball stage (238°). Remove from the stove and beat until creamy and of spreading consistency, adding cream or milk a teaspoon at a time if the mixture is too thick. Frost the cake immediately.

MAKES ONE 10-INCH TUBE CAKE OR
ONE 3-TIERED, 8-INCH LAYER CAKE

PEANUT CAULIFLOWER WIENER CASSEROLE

1 *medium cauliflower, separated into flowerets*
1 *cup chopped green pepper*
$^1/_2$ *cup sliced onion*
2 *cups chopped wieners or hot dogs*
3 *tablespoons butter*
3 *tablespoons flour*
$1^1/_2$ *cups milk*
1 *cup grated sharp Cheddar cheese*
$^1/_2$ *teaspoon salt*
Dash of pepper
Dash of hot pepper sauce
$^1/_2$ *cup chopped peanuts*
Pimiento strips

Cook the cauliflower, green pepper, and onion in a small amount of boiling salted water for about 10 minutes, or until the cauliflower is barely tender. Drain, combine with the wieners, and arrange in a greased $1^1/_2$-quart casserole.

Preheat the oven at 350°. In a saucepan, melt the butter and blend in the flour. Add the milk gradually and bring to a boil, stirring, and cook 1 minute, or until thickened. Remove from the heat and stir in $^3/_4$ cup of the grated cheese, the salt, pepper, and hot pepper sauce. Pour over the top of the cauliflower mixture. Sprinkle with the chopped peanuts. Bake for 25 minutes. Sprinkle with the remaining $^1/_4$ cup grated cheese, and bake 5 minutes longer. If a browned top is desired, run under the broiler a minute or two. Garnish with pimiento strips.

MAKES 4 TO 6 SERVINGS

PRIZEWINNING PEANUT BUTTER

$2^1/_2$ *cups roasted peanuts (after husks have been removed)*
$^1/_4$ *cup peanut oil*
$^1/_4$ *teaspoon salt*
1 *teaspoon sugar*
1 *tablespoon honey*

Grind the peanuts in a food grinder two or three times, using the finest blade, or put through a food processor until they are pulverized. For crunchy-type peanut butter, a few of the peanuts may be ground coarsely.

In a small saucepan, combine the peanut oil, salt, sugar, and honey, and heat until warm, making sure the mixture does not become hot, which tends to harden the peanut butter. Combine the ground peanuts and the warm oil mixture in a bowl, mixing thoroughly. Pack into a 1-pint jar.

MAKES 2 CUPS

Festival Facts

The National Peanut Festival, which began in 1945, is held annually for one week in mid-October in Dothan, Alabama. Dothan is on U.S. Highway 84 in southeast Alabama. For further information, write: The National Peanut Festival, P.O. Box 976, Dothan, Alabama 36301.

Kutztown Pennsylvania Dutch Folk Festival

25

Kutztown, Pennsylvania

"The last word for food freaks" or "a gourmand's paradise" are not exaggerated descriptions of the Kutztown Pennsylvania Dutch Folk Festival. At this food-eating-festival-to-end-all-food-eating festivals, one can spend the entire day trying to eat a little of everything, and still not succeed.

The names of some of the dishes are intriguing in themselves: funnel cakes, for example, or other sweet treats such as cinnamon flop, bear claw buns, and shoofly pie. There's rather an Alice-in-Wonderland quality to a few of the names—potato filling, for instance, which doesn't fill anything except the eater, and chicken pot pie, which isn't really a pie at all, but more like a chicken stew simmered with large homemade noodle squares.

A wide range of specialties is sold at the many food booths scattered throughout the festival. Birch beer, cherry fritters, sticky buns, chicken corn soup, sausage sandwiches, plowlines (a fried pastry), funnel cakes with powdered sugar or molasses, corn on the cob, and big, soft pretzels—perhaps one of the most widely known Pennsylvania Dutch foods—can all be tasted.

But perhaps the best way to get a well-rounded sampling of Pennsylvania Dutch cooking is to sit down with a group at a long table in one of the food pavilions (actually huge tents) for a "set-out" of food. The entire meal, except dessert, is put out at once at these family-style dinners made and served by various church and Grange groups from the area. While the people who operate these pavilions obviously do a lot of hard work to produce the meals they do, their manner remains relaxed, their faces open and friendly, and their sense of cooperation and team spirit enviable. At the tent of the Women's Guild of Zion's United Church of Christ of Windsor Castle, Pennsylvania, as many as 150 church members turn out about 2,500 dinners daily.

From the youngest to the oldest, everyone has a job to do. Children six or seven years old help to stack up dishes, older girls wait on tables, older boys fetch and carry, and adults prepare food. Often they stay up long into the night, with the men baking hams and frying chickens and the women baking cakes and pies for the following day. Oldsters earn the sit-down jobs of peeling, cutting, and chopping the vegetables that form part of a typical meal that includes baked ham, chicken, dumplings and apples, celery and carrot sticks, pepper salad (a kind of a coleslaw), cottage cheese and apple butter (a strange-sounding but delicious-tasting combination), pickled beets, potato filling, corn, pickles, and green beans. These foods are dished up in big bowls or on huge platters carried in by aproned, bonneted girls, and the portions are generous. To make certain that you're filled up, the price of the dinner includes a dessert like sweet lemon-strip pie or milk tart.

Even before the fair begins, hundreds of gallons of chowchow, pickled red beets, and other relishes have been made up by members of the church groups. Mrs. Paul J. Miller of the

Zion group, whose family has been helping to feed visitors at the festival for more that twenty-five years, calculates that in a typical year at the fair thirty Zion people make up about 165 gallons of chowchow alone to serve at their dinners. Numbers are impressive here, and one admires the teamwork among people who are restaurateurs only eight days out of each year in serving 1,000 pounds of ham along with 1,500 pounds of chicken and all the side dishes in a single day.

It would not be amiss to walk around the festival grounds after a "set-out" to see a few of the food-related events. Things to look for are the outdoor bake oven, the herb garden with its fresh herbs growing and its dried ones hanging in preparation for winter use, the Grange displays of tidily bottled home-canned foods, the potato-candy maker, the mush maker, the sauerkraut maker, the apple crusher, cider maker, and apple-butter boilers. In the farmers' market are local cheeses, Lebanon bologna, ponhaws (scrapple), baked goods, and other items to take home.

For those who have an interest in Pennsylvania Dutch cooking or those newly introduced to the cuisine and curious about it, there is a unique Country Kitchen to visit. Built out-of-doors and completely open on one side to allow for observation, it is a replica of an old-fashioned and quite charming Pennsylvania Dutch kitchen. Here a small group of women demonstrate the skill and experience they have developed in their many years of preparing regional dishes. Since cooking is done over a wood-burning iron stove, each festival day begins early with fire-building chores for Mary Redcay, who is in charge of the kitchen and all the planning it involves. Mary Sise and the other dedicated ladies of the Country Kitchen join her a little later in the morning. Working in a homelike atmosphere, they fix an entire meal at the corncob-and-wood-burning stove, including bread and other baked goods. The dinner they prepare is served in the late afternoon to the day's selection of lucky festival craftsmen and workers seated around a large oval wooden table where all can see the "set-out." While the ladies cook and bake, they chat pleasantly with festival visitors, answer questions about their work, pass out copies of the day's menu along with a recipe, and otherwise do all they can to share their knowledge of Pennsylvania Dutch cooking.

Since Pennsylvania Dutch cooking is farm cooking, it's hearty fare, and neither at the Country Kitchen nor anywhere else at the festival is much thought given to calorie counting or waistline watching. Sturdy foods are needed by farmers who work outdoors for long hours every day, and this is reflected in the generous use of butter and fats, milk and cream, sugar and starches. Noodle and potato dishes abound, as do sweets and baked goods, and no meal is complete without a dessert. Molasses, cider vinegar, celery seed, and sometimes saffron are typical flavorings used. Meats lean toward those obtained from animals raised on local farms, with chicken, pork, ham, bacon, and sausage ranking high. Beautiful farm-fresh vegetables are served, often in combination with each other (peas, celery, and carrots steamed together and served with butter, for example) or with flavorings of crumbled bacon or fried onions, and there are many pickled vegetables, too. Sparkling glass jars of bright relishes, pickles, and vegetables displayed at the Country Kitchen and other places throughout the fair show how these products are preserved for winter use.

The women who cook throughout the Kutztown festival say that there has been very little change in Pennsylvania Dutch cooking over the years. Some can trace recipes back for eight generations, and directions are more likely to be kept in their heads than written down on paper. But these recipes are freely repeated to festival-goers by the women who enjoy sharing the pleasures of "fressing" (eating).

Friendliness and a willingness to share are typical of the people who participate in the entire festival, and their specialties are not limited to cooking. Myriad crafts and skills are represented on thirty-five acres of activity. An average of twenty-four thousand people daily during the eight days of the festival watch demonstrations of pitching hay, raising barns, shearing sheep, spinning flax, making sunbonnets, working with wood, copper, and pewter, boiling soap, painting hex signs, making candles, weaving, lacemaking, wool dyeing, and roof thatching, to name just a few.

Special and out-of-the-ordinary crafts are worth seeking out. For example, scratch-carved eggs are made by Barbara Bomberger. Dyes for her unusual work are made from natural substances such as blueberries, spinach, and onion skins. The eggs she decorates by scratching off the color to create designs range in size from tiny wild bird eggs to those of giant ostriches, with goose, duck, or chicken eggs, the most popular, falling somewhere between the two extremes. Some of them are made for hanging, others are pierced and suspended from chains to be worn as necklaces, and still others are made with hinged doors that swing open to reveal miniature fairyland scenes.

In the quilting building there are literally hundreds of beautiful handmade quilts displayed for prize competition and sale at almost too-low prices, and there are farmers' markets and antique shops, hoedowns, Amish wedding simulations, one-room schoolhouses, smokehouses, outhouses, and icehouses, endless plays, pageants, and entertainments, and daily seminars on customs, traditions, crafts, and other facets of Pennsylvania Dutch life.

All of this began more that twenty-five years ago when three college professors from Franklin and Marshall College organized the first Kutztown Festival as a sort of outgrowth from the Pennsylvania Dutch Folklore Center which they had set up. The purpose of the Center then, as now, as well as the purpose of the Kutztown Festival, is to bring knowledge of the Pennsylvania Germans and their rural culture to others.

It should be noted that although there are portrayals of the Amish way of life at the festival, the activities for the most part represent and are run by the "worldly" Dutch. These are the Lutheran and Reformed church groups who accept the world and its ways, in contrast to the Amish and other "plain people" who prefer to remain apart and to live more in the manner of past generations.

Dorothy Miller has contributed the recipe for Grumbiere Filsil, or Potato Filling, a scaled-down version of that served by the Zion people. From Country Kitchen's Mary Redcay comes her great-grandmother's recipe for Lettuce with Bacon Dressing, and her grandmother's recipe for Cinnamon Flop, along with the comment that children like this "shleck" (anything sweet). Also from Mary Redcay are the recipes for Chicken Corn Soup, Shin Beef with Marrow Beans and Potatoes, Red Beet Eggs, Cracker Pudding, and Chicken Pot Pie. Mary Sise has contributed her recipe for Leb Cookies, and from one of the Country Kitchen's daily menu and recipe handouts comes the recipe for Hutzel Brie. Finally, Anna Henry shares her recipe for Funnel Cakes.

POTATO FILLING

1 cup chopped onions
3 tablespoons butter or margarine
3 slices stale bread, cut into cubes
1 quart mashed potatoes (preferably hot)
1 egg, beaten
1 cup milk
$^1/_3$ cup finely chopped parsley
1 teaspoon flour
$^1/_4$ teaspoon sugar
Pepper to taste

Preheat the oven at 400°. Sauté the onions in the butter or margarine until soft, adding the bread cubes partway through the sautéeing. Combine the mixture with the mashed potatoes. Combine the egg and milk, and add gradually to the potato mixture. Add the remaining ingredients and turn into a buttered $1^1/_2$-quart baking dish. Bake until it has heated through and the top has browned, about 30 minutes.

MAKES 8 SERVINGS

LETTUCE WITH BACON DRESSING

1 head lettuce
1 small onion, finely chopped
3 eggs
$^3/_4$ cup sugar
$^3/_4$ cup water
$^1/_2$ cup cider vinegar
$^1/_2$ pound bacon cut crosswise into 1-inch lengths
2 tablespoons flour

Wash, dry, and cut up the lettuce, and combine with the onion. Beat the eggs, and add the sugar, water, and vinegar. Fry the bacon until crisp, and stir in the flour. Add the egg mixture to the frying pan, bring to a boil, and cook, stirring, until the mixture thickens. Pour over the lettuce and onions, toss, and serve immediately.

MAKES 4 TO 6 SERVINGS

CINNAMON FLOP

1 *heaping tablespoon soft butter*
1 *cup sugar*
2 *cups flour*
Pinch of salt
2 *teaspoons baking powder*
Pinch of allspice
1 *cup milk*
$^1/_4$ *cup dark-brown sugar*
$^1/_2$ *teaspoon cinnamon*
$^1/_4$ *teaspoon nutmeg*
1 *tablespoon butter*

Preheat the oven at 325°. Cream the butter and add the sugar. Sift together and add the flour, salt, baking powder, and allspice alternately with the milk. Pour into a greased 9-inch-square baking pan. Combine the dark brown sugar, cinnamon, and nutmeg, and sprinkle over the top. Dot with the butter. Poke the butter down into the batter with a finger. Bake about 25 minutes. Serve from the pan.

MAKES 9 OR 16 SERVINGS

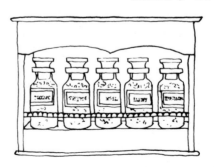

CHICKEN CORN SOUP

1 *four-pound stewing chicken, whole*
1 *tablespoon salt*
Pepper to taste
1 *onion, cut in half*
2 *ribs celery, chopped*
$^1/_2$ *pound narrow noodles*
1 *seventeen-ounce can creamed corn*
1 *twelve-ounce can whole-kernel corn*
2 *or* 3 *hard-cooked eggs, sliced*
Pinch of saffron (optional)
1 *tablespoon chopped parsley*

Cover the chicken with water, bring slowly to a boil, and skim until particles no longer rise to the surface. Add the salt, pepper, onion, and celery. Simmer 1 hour, or until the chicken is tender. Remove the chicken from the pot and cut into serving pieces, removing bones and visible cartilage.

Meanwhile, add the noodles to the pot and boil until tender. Add the creamed corn and whole-kernel corn, along with the cut-up chicken, hard-cooked eggs, saffron, and parsley. Heat thoroughly and serve in soup bowls.

MAKES ABOUT 8 SERVINGS

SHIN BEEF WITH MARROW BEANS AND POTATOES

1 *pound marrow beans*
2 *slices shin beef with round bone in (total weight* $2^1/_2$ *to* 3 *pounds)*
1 *tablespoon salt*
Pepper to taste
1 *onion, chopped*
6 *carrots, scraped and sliced*
2 *or* 3 *ribs celery, cut into 1-inch lengths*
1 *tablespoon chopped parsley*
4 *to* 6 *potatoes, peeled and cut into* $^1/_2$-*inch slices*

Soak the beans overnight or for 8 hours in cold water to cover by several inches.

Place the beef in a large pot with cold water to cover. Bring to a boil, lower the heat to simmer, and skim until no more particles rise to the surface. Add the salt, pepper, and onion, and simmer, covered, 30 minutes. Add the soaked, drained beans and simmer 1 hour. Add the carrots, celery, and parsley, and continue cooking 30 minutes longer. Add the potatoes and cook until all the vegetables are tender. Remove the bones and any pieces of fat, and break up the meat if it is still in large sections. Arrange the meat and vegetables on a large, deep platter.

MAKES 8 TO 10 SERVINGS

RED BEET EGGS

12 eggs
1 can sliced beets (reserve liquid)
1/2 cup vinegar
1/2 cup sugar
Salt and pepper to taste
1/8 teaspoon celery seed
1/8 teaspoon allspice

Hard-cook the eggs, remove the shells, and set aside.

Place the beets, vinegar, 1/2 cup of the liquid from the beets (adding water, if necessary, to make 1/2 cup), sugar, salt, pepper, celery seed, and allspice in a saucepan. Bring to a boil. Remove from the flame, and pour into a bowl. Add the eggs and allow to cool. Cover and refrigerate at least 24 hours before serving, turning the eggs once or twice during that time.

MAKES 12 SERVINGS

CRACKER PUDDING
(A Dessert)

> *Crackers (such as Saltines or similar type)*
> 1 *quart milk*
> 1 *cup sugar*
> $^1/_2$ *cup shredded coconut*
> 1 *teaspoon vanilla extract*
> 2 *eggs, beaten*

Roll over enough crackers with a rolling pin to make 1 cup cracker crumbs. Scald the milk. Add the cracker crumbs, sugar, coconut, and vanilla extract to the milk. Stir a little of this mixture into the eggs, then add the eggs to the cracker-crumb mixture. Bring to a boil, lower the heat, and simmer 5 minutes, stirring occasionally. Pour into a serving dish. Cool and chill.

MAKES 8 SERVINGS

CHICKEN POT PIE

> 1 *four-pound stewing chicken, whole*
> 1 *tablespoon salt*
> *Pepper to taste*
> *Generous pinch of saffron*
> 2 *onions, chopped*
> 3 *ribs celery, chopped*
> 2 *cups flour*
> *Pinch of salt*
> *Pinch of baking powder*
> 2 *eggs*
> $^1/_3$ *cup milk (approximately)*

Cover the chicken with cold water, bring slowly to a boil, and skim until no more particles rise to the surface. Add the salt, pepper, saffron, onions, and celery. Lower the heat and simmer, partially covered, about 30 minutes or until the chicken is tender. Remove the chicken from the pot. If necessary, add enough boiling water to the pot to make 2 quarts of liquid.

Meanwhile, sift together into a bowl the flour, salt, and baking powder. Make a well in the center and add the eggs and $1/3$ cup milk. Mix until thoroughly blended, adding a little more milk if necessary to make a dough firm enough to roll out. Roll out very thinly on a lightly floured board, and cut into 2x3-inch rectangles.

After the chicken has been removed from the pot, drop the noodle squares, one by one, into the boiling broth, a layer at a time. When all the noodles are cooking, lower the heat, cover, and simmer 30 minutes.

Meanwhile, cut the chicken into serving pieces, removing the skin and bones if desired, and add to the pot 10 minutes before the end of the cooking time.

MAKES ABOUT 8 SERVINGS

LEB COOKIES

6 tablespoons lard
6 tablespoons butter
$1^{1}/_{2}$ pounds ($4^{1}/_{2}$ cups) light-brown sugar
1 small egg, beaten
$1/_{2}$ teaspoon hartshorn salt*
1 tablespoon baking soda
2 cups buttermilk
8 cups flour
$1/_{2}$ teaspoon salt
1 egg, beaten

Cream together the lard and butter. Gradually add the light-brown sugar. Add the small egg. Combine the hartshorn salt and baking soda, and add to the buttermilk. Sift together the flour and salt and add to the butter-sugar-egg mixture alternately with the buttermilk mixture. Combine well. Cover and re-frigerate 8 hours or overnight.

Preheat the oven at 350°. Drop the dough by spoonsful onto

---

*Also called ammonium carbonate. May be purchased at drugstores.

an ungreased baking sheet and brush with the beaten egg. Bake about 12 minutes. Cool on a wire rack. Mary Sise calls these "good dunking cookies."

MAKES 4 OR 5 DOZEN

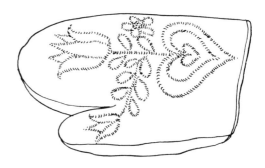

HUTZEL BRIE
(A Dried-Fruit Dessert)

> 1 *cup dried apricots*
> 1 *cup dried pears*
> 1 *cup dried peaches*
> 1 *cup prunes*
> $1/2$ *cup schnitz (dried apples)*
> $1/2$ *cup raisins*
> $1/2$ *cup dried or canned cherries**
> 2 *tablespoons brown sugar (or to taste)*
> *Juice and grated rind of 1 lemon*

Place dried fruits in a bowl and cover with cold water. Soak for 30 minutes. Drain. Place in a saucepan, adding fresh cold water just to cover and the brown sugar. Bring to a boil, lower the heat, and simmer, partially covered, 30 minutes. Add the lemon juice and rind. Cool and chill.

MAKES 8 OR MORE SERVINGS

---

*If using canned sweet cherries, add 5 minutes before the end of the cooking time. If using canned sour cherries, add along with the dried fruits. In either case, juice from the canned cherries may be substituted for part of the water used to cook the fruits.

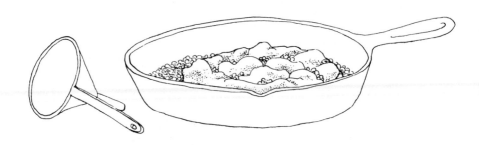

FUNNEL CAKES

2 eggs
2 cups milk
2 tablespoons sugar
3 cups flour
2 teaspoons baking powder
1 teaspoon salt
Lard for frying
Confectioner's sugar or molasses

Beat the eggs, add the milk and sugar, and mix well. Sift together the flour, baking powder, and salt, and add to the egg mixture.

Melt enough lard to measure about 2 inches in a deep skillet, and heat to 375°. Hold a finger over the end of a funnel (one with a long handle if you have it) and pour ¹/₂ cup or so of the batter into the funnel. Controlling the flow of batter with the finger, allow it to flow in an uneven circular pattern into the hot lard, starting from the center and working outward. Fry the cake until lightly browned, turn it with tongs, and brown the other side. Each side should take about 2 minutes. Lower the heat if the cakes brown too quickly. Drain on paper towels. Continue frying until all the batter has been used.

Sift confectioner's sugar over the funnel cakes or pour molasses over them. Eat them while still warm, or serve them cold. Anna Henry says you can eat them for breakfast, lunch, with coffee, at a picnic, on the beach, or anytime.

MAKES ABOUT 1 DOZEN

Festival Facts

The Kutztown Pennsylvania Dutch Folk Festival, which began in 1950, is held annually for eight days beginning on the Saturday prior to July 4 at the festival grounds in Kutztown, Pennsylvania. Kutztown, located between Allentown and Reading, is reached by taking U.S. 22 (Interstate 78), exiting at Krumsville and taking Route 737 south to Kutztown, or by taking the Pennsylvania Turnpike and taking U.S. 222 at the Reading Interchange north to Kutztown. For further information, write: Pennsylvania Folklife Society, College Boulevard and Vine, Kutztown, Pennsylvania 19530.

Persimmon Festival

26

Mitchell, Indiana

Pucker up! It's persimmon time in Mitchell, Indiana, when persimmon lovers gather to nibble on persimmon goodies, enter persuasive puddings in the festival's most popular competition, the Persimmon Pudding Contest, or try the equally challenging Novelty Persimmon Dessert Contest. Cookie or cupcake mavens hasten to bring their special entries to Persimmon Cookie or Cupcake Contests arty enough to be ranked as categories of the Arts and Crafts Show.

Actually, as people at the festival, who probably know more about persimmons than people anywhere else in the United States, explain, you shouldn't have to pucker up when you eat a persimmon. If you do, it means you're eating an unripe fruit that still contains a large quantity of tannin, the substance that causes the constrictive characteristic of the fruit. A good, ripe Indiana persimmon, like all persimmons, should be soft, sweet, and delectable, and is considered the choicest of fruits in the southern part of the state, where persimmon trees grow wild in fence rows, on country farms, and in cultivated orchards. One of these orchards is known to be a good seventy-five years old.

What is almost certain to be the world's only persimmon-pulp canning factory is also located in southern Indiana, in Mitchell, and it supplies canned fruit pulp the year round to those who can't wait from one harvest to another to enjoy the unusual fruit.

Persimmons look a little like tomatoes, in that their shape is round and their skin is smooth, but here the similarity ends, for the color can range from the most commonly seen orange to an actual black, the shape varies (with some fruits round and other narrowing toward the base), and the flavor and texture are completely unrelated to those of the tomato. The stem end of a persimmon is large and round and circled by a wreath of flat, narrow leaves, one of its most easily recognizable identification marks.

In September and October the harvesters of Mitchell pick the fruits and ship them off to be enjoyed fresh in other parts of the United States, reserving enough for themselves to eat as is or to make into persimmon pulp for persimmon puddings and other local specialties. Most persimmon recipes call for persimmon pulp, which is best prepared by washing, stemming, and quartering the soft fruit, scooping the pulp from the skin with a spoon, and putting it through a sieve, food mill, electric blender, or food processor. Another way to get persimmon pulp, especially when the fresh fruit is out of season, is to use the canned product put out by the Mitchell company with the cheery name of Dymple's Delight Persimmon Products. It's unlikely you'll see this product on your grocer's shelf, but you can write to the firm at Route 2, Box 146, Mitchell, Indiana 47446, for prices and details.

Should you want to try your hand at a persimmon pudding to enter in the festival's annual contest, it's reassuring to know that while only one entry per person is accepted, there's no discrimination as to age, sex, or place of residence, and you can sign up as late as the final day of the festival. But be prepared to compete with perhaps three hundred or more pudding makers, each convinced that his or hers is the best pudding going. According to the experts, a good persimmon pudding should have a smooth, glossy top, and it is first judged on its appearance, evenness of texture, and uniformity of color, which can be dark or light depending on whether sweet milk or buttermilk has been used as an ingredient.

The entries, all of which must consist of a six-inch square of unadorned pudding on a paper plate covered by transparent wrap, pass through the first judging (and there are as many as thirty judges at work), and those that make it to this point are then considered for taste. The goal is to have a pudding that has a distinct persimmon flavor unmasked by excess spices or other flavorings, and then you may find yourself walking away with the first prize of a hundred dollars or more. One of the prizewinners, Joan Buher, whose pudding recipe appears below, uses a subtle flavoring of only half a teaspoon each of vanilla extract and cinnamon. Twice a winner of the Persimmon Pudding Contest, Mrs. Buher sticks to the culinary part of the festival and leaves to her daughter, Patrice, the winning of other titles such as Persimmon Festival Queen, as she did recently.

People who like to make persimmon bread, persimmon rolls, various persimmon desserts, or persimmon puddings with whipped cream or other toppings can enter the Novelty Persimmon Dessert Contest. A good example of the variety of entries is the prizewinning recipe for Persimmon Brownies by Jill Green, which is included below.

If you don't feel like it, there's no reason you have to cook or bake at all to enjoy the Persimmon Festival, since you can buy persimmon puddings and other persimmon treats all made up and ready to go. There's a booth that makes a special persimmon ice cream, and other foods and snacks are available.

Persimmons are represented in nonedible forms, too, as in the Arts and Crafts Show, where all sorts of decorative items are made from the seeds of locally grown persimmons. During some festivals there are quilts and afghans on display, designed and made by local residents, each creation using persimmon fruits or boughs in their pattern in some form.

A fixture at the festival, eagerly awaited from year to year by many persimmon-proud Indiana residents, is the Persimmon Fruit and Nut Show. People comb their orchards, fields, and backyards to bring in the best persimmon specimens they can find for judging, and those whose interests lie more in the world of nuts engage in a similar hunt to enter specimens of native Indiana nuts in the competition. None of the nuts comes from commercial orchards, since there are said to be no commercially grown nuts in the state, but the hobbyists bring in their own homegrown hickory nuts, pecans, chestnuts, filberts, Carpathian walnuts, buckeyes, and certain acorns, along with questions on Indiana nut culture to be answered by the experts on hand.

The eight-day Persimmon Festival begins with a candlelight tour of its nearby pioneer village, as well as the traditional Persimmon Ball on the same evening. The following days bring a variety of diversions that include an Arts and Crafts Show where sourdough-bread making, corn-bread making, apple-butter making, and other old-time food preparations are demonstrated, an art exhibit, a hobby and flea market, commercial and industrial exhibits, a Persimmon Parade, carnival, teen dance, square dance, and evening entertainment on the town's Main Street stage.

You may not find such things at the festival, but next time you're in the market for golf clubs ask the salesman what kind of wood was used in making the golf club heads. Chances are, you'll find that it's persimmon, an extremely dense, hard wood that's highly resistant to mechanical shock. Since persimmon trees grow to be some fifty feet high, there's material for a lot of golf club heads when one of the trees meets with some misfortune such as a tornado—as now and then happens in Mitchell—and falls to the ground.

JOAN'S HUNDRED-DOLLAR PERSIMMON PUDDING

2 cups persimmon pulp
2 cups sugar
3 eggs, beaten
1 teaspoon baking soda
1$^1/_2$ cups buttermilk
1$^1/_2$ cups flour
1 teaspoon baking powder
$^1/_8$ teaspoon salt
$^1/_2$ teaspoon vanilla extract
$^1/_2$ teaspoon cinnamon
$^1/_4$ cup cream
$^1/_4$ cup butter

Preheat the oven at 350°. Combine the persimmon pulp and sugar. Add the eggs and mix well. Dissolve the baking soda in the buttermilk. Sift together the flour, baking powder, and salt, and add to the batter alternately with the buttermilk. Stir in the vanilla extract, cinnamon, and cream.

Melt the butter in a 9x13-inch baking pan, and pour the melted butter into the batter, leaving just enough to coat the bottom and sides of the baking pan. Beat the batter well. Pour into the baking pan and smooth with a rubber spatula. Bake about 1 hour until nicely browned.

MAKES ABOUT 10 SERVINGS

PERSIMMON BROWNIES

FOR THE BROWNIES:
$^1/_2$ cup butter
2 cups sugar
2 cups persimmon pulp
1 cup buttermilk
3 eggs
2 cups flour

1 *teaspoon baking powder*
1 *teaspoon baking soda*
1 *teaspoon cinnamon*
1 *teaspoon nutmeg*

FOR THE ICING:
  1 *three-ounce package cream cheese*
  $^{1}/_{4}$ *cup butter*
  1 *teaspoon vanilla extract*
  2 *tablespoons cream*
  1 *pound confectioner's sugar, sifted*
  1 *cup chopped pecans*

FOR THE BROWNIES: Preheat the oven at 350°. Cream the butter, add the sugar, and mix well. Add the persimmon pulp, buttermilk, and eggs. Sift together the remaining ingredients and add to the persimmon mixture. Turn into a greased 9x13- or 10x12-inch baking pan and bake 35 to 40 minutes. Cool on a wire rack.

FOR THE ICING: Cream together the cream cheese and butter until smooth. Add the vanilla extract and cream, and mix well. Add the confectioner's sugar gradually, mixing well. Spread on the cooled brownies. Sprinkle with chopped pecans. Cut into squares.

MAKES 12 SERVINGS

Festival Facts

The Persimmon Festival, which began in 1947, is held annually during the last full week in September, beginning and ending on a Saturday, in Mitchell, Indiana, which is one mile west of Route 37, about thirty-five miles south of Bloomington. For further information, write: Mrs. Betty Mather, Secretary, Mitchell Chamber of Commerce, Mitchell, Indiana 47446.

27

Pittsburgh, Pennsylvania

It doesn't take eighty days to go around the world if you travel via the Pittsburgh Folk Festival. Here in a matter of a few hours you can travel from Croatia to China, from Ireland to Italy, or from Slovenia to Scandinavia.

In all, about twenty nations are represented, each group made up of some of the ethnic peoples whose forebears built the city of Pittsburgh, and who now live in and around the area. The theme of the festival, which is as much an educational as a civic event, is Unity in Diversity, and the thirty-five hundred people who work harmoniously to make the festival a reality attest to the fact that the theme is a workable one.

Each group erects two booths, one for the preparation and sale of its most tantalizing national dishes, and the other for the display of its crafts and Old World treasures. These booths form an international marketplace where the festival visitor can feast his senses from five P.M. to midnight during any or all of the three nights the event is held. The melodies of strolling musicians please the ear, while foods made from treasured family recipes delight the palate. The eye is charmed by bright peasant costumes, ancestral heirlooms, embroideries and tapestries, filigree jewelry, mosaics, musical instruments, copper- and brasswork, woodwork, and demonstrations of folk crafts in the display booths. The coronation cups of Nicholas II and Alexandra are shown by the Russian group, for example, while the Lebanese include copper proverb trays among their artifacts. The Bulgarians let you sniff their special attar of roses, the Chinese demonstrate their deftness at calligraphy and brush painting, and the English feature a collection of formidable medieval weaponry.

Each evening at eight o'clock, six or seven of the nations participate in a two-hour program of native dances and songs accompanied by live music, so that during the three nights of the festival each nation is represented on the stage. Costumes are striking and authentic, as are the performances, ranging from harvest celebrations to wedding and war dances.

Having sampled some of the dishes before showtime, one hopes to have room for more after the evening's performance, but it is difficult to decide whether to try all the specialties from one country or to pick and choose a bit from each of several countries.

The Bulgarians tempt one with their menu of musaka (eggplant casserole), oris i gubi (rice and mushrooms), kebapchita (hamburger with plain bread), salata (tossed salad), banitza (strudel with cheese, spinach, or leeks), torte ot orihi (nut torte), and kosolo miejko (yogurt). The Chinese offer everything from eggrolls to fortune cookies, while the Germans include knackwurst, bratwurst, sauerkraut, and spaetzle on their menu, the English feature roast beef, the Latvians offer dzervenu sula (a cranberry punch), and the Slovenians make flancati (twisted crispies to please the sweet tooth).

The most popular foods seem to be potato pancakes, pizza, and pirogi, with eggrolls and Philippine-style chicken close runners-up, but there's no need to skip the more exotic offerings. Included on the menus, which vary little from year to year, one can find Bulgarian gyuvech (a meat-and-vegetable casserole), Croatian grah i kasa juha (bean-and-barley soup), Greek soutzoukakia me pilafi (meatballs in wine sauce and rice), Hungarian palacsinta turos (cheese pancakes), Irish aranac mulsirum (breaded mushrooms), Israeli falafel (fried chick-peas served in Middle Eastern bread topped with salad and sesame sauce), Latvian kumpis (ham baked in rye dough), Lithuanian kugelis (baked grated potatoes), and Slovakian ceregy ("celestial curlers," a cookie), to name only a few.

Besides serving their food specialties, many of the national groups also put on cooking demonstrations in their food booths and provide recipes to the onlookers.

The craft booths are often food-oriented, too, as when the Irish devote their display to table settings of Belleek china, Waterford glass, and Irish linen, the Scandinavians feature a traditional Scandinavian home kitchen with gleaming white corner fireplace, copper cooking utensils, and wooden, glass, and pewter accessories, and the Serbians show what a typical kitchen would look like in their homeland.

Sponsored by Robert Morris College, and begun in 1956 by a sister institution of that college, the festival now attracts thirty-five to forty thousand visitors each year and is certainly one of Pittsburgh's most outstanding events.

The recipes that follow are for Bulgarian Gyuvech and Lithuanian Kugelis.

BULGARIAN GYUVECH
(Meat-and-Vegetable Casserole)

> 2 *pounds beef, cubed*
> 4 *carrots, scraped and sliced*
> 2 *ribs celery, sliced*
> $^1/_4$ *head cabbage, thinly sliced*
> 2 *potatoes, peeled and cubed*
> $^1/_2$ *cup green beans, cut in 1-inch lengths*
> 1 *onion, cut in pieces*

Salt and pepper to taste
1$^1/_2$ *cups tomato juice*

Preheat the oven at 350°. Mix together the beef, carrots, celery, cabbage, potatoes, green beans, onion, salt, and pepper, and turn into a greased 9x12x2-inch baking pan. Pour the tomato juice over the top of the mixture. Cover with foil and bake 2$^1/_2$ hours.

MAKES 6 TO 8 SERVINGS

LITHUANIAN KUGELIS
(Baked Grated Potatoes)

$^1/_3$ *pound bacon, cut up*
1 *large onion, chopped*
4$^1/_2$ *to 5 pounds potatoes, peeled*
2 *eggs*
2 *teaspoons salt (or to taste)*
Cottage cheese or sour cream (optional)

Preheat the oven at 325°. Sauté the bacon and onions together until the onions are soft. Grate the potatoes and drain them well in a colander. Place them in a bowl and combine with the eggs and salt. Add the bacon-and-onion mixture, with most of the bacon drippings. Blend well and pour into a greased 2$^1/_2$-quart baking dish. Bake 1$^1/_2$ to 2 hours until a rich brown. Serve plain or with cottage cheese or sour cream.

MAKES 12 SERVINGS

Festival Facts

The Pittsburgh Folk Festival, which began in 1956, is held annually for three nights in late May at the Civic Arena in Pittsburgh, Pennsylvania. Pittsburgh can be reached from all major roads in southwestern Pennsylvania. For further information, write: Pittsburgh Folk Festival, 610 Fifth Avenue, Pittsburgh, Pennsylvania 15219.

Potato Feast Day and Maine Potato Blossom Festival

28

Fort Fairfield, Maine

In July the potato fields surrounding Houlton, Maine, are a mass of delicate pink, mauve, and white flowers, and the townsfolk choose this loveliest time of the year to hold their annual feast in honor of the famous Maine potato. Houlton, which is located at the southern tip of Aroostook County's potato-growing area, has a one-day celebration where the citizenry sets up booths to dispense numerous prepared-at-home potato dishes made by people who really know their spuds. Potatoburgers, potato yeast rolls, potato dessert cake, and even potato candy are some of the specialties, and there are barbecued chickens and other fill-ins to be had, too.

Houltonites know their potato sacks, as well as what fills them, and one of the feast day events is a Potato Sack Fashion Contest, with entrants making complete outfits from potato sacks. These ticklish garments run the gamut from potato sack overalls to fringed shorts and vests, belted dresses, and evening gowns worn with white gloves. Other events of the day include sidewalk sales, ice cream sales, wagon rides, flea markets, antique shows, arts and crafts shows, and an evening square dance in the street.

For those interested in the great out-of-doors as well as potato feasting, it's worth noting that Houlton is only a few miles from the Allagash Wilderness Waterway, one of the last great wilderness areas in the Northeast. This unique ninety-two-mile corridor of waterways includes lakes, rapids, waterfalls, a feeling of peace and tranquillity, and a challenge to true outdoor-loving canoeists. For details on how to gain access to the waterway and prepare for a trip through all or part of it, one should write to the Bureau of Parks and Recreation, Augusta, Maine 04330.

Forty-five miles north of Houlton, the town of Fort Fairfield holds its Maine Potato Blossom Festival, a four-day tribute to the Maine tuber, a few weeks after its neighbor's Potato Feast Day. Saturday's parade features a bevy of beautiful Potato Queen contestants, as well as the floats and bands one expects to see at such an event. But from the city folks' point of view, one interesting part of the parade is the mass of potato-farming equipment that moves along down the street. Huge plows, tractors, and potato diggers, and other grand-sized equipment follow the route of march, some driven by men and some by women in recent years. These tremendous and, to the outsider, strange-appearing pieces of farm machinery have been instrumental in making Maine's potato industry the giant one that it is, and the parade a noteworthy one.

Potato-picking contests, or sometimes potato-peeling contests in which Maine politicians compete with one another in the quick removal of potato skins, sports, chapel singing, skydiving, and horse shows are some of the diverse events that are scheduled during the Potato Blossom Festival. One should try to attend the traditional Spud Supper put on annually by the Aroostook County Granges. Here the potato appears in an expanse of dishes that include old-time-favorite potatoes au gratin, scalloped potatoes with ham, and a variety of potato salads, of which Blue Cheese Potato Salad (recipe follows) is one of the more unusual.

The other recipes below are from the Houlton Potato Feast and include sturdy Potatoburgers, Potato Yeast Rolls, and rich Potato Fudge.

BLUE CHEESE POTATO SALAD

> *4 cups Maine potatoes, peeled and diced*
> *1 cup celery, diced*
> *3 tablespoons onion, minced*
> *¹/₂ cup mayonnaise*
> *¹/₂ cup bottled blue cheese salad dressing*
> *Salt and pepper to taste*
> *2 hard-cooked eggs, sliced*
> *Parsley sprigs*

Cook the diced potatoes in boiling salted water until tender. Drain and chill. Combine with the celery and onion. Mix the mayonnaise and blue cheese salad dressing together and add to the potato mixture along with the salt and pepper. Add the egg slices, saving some for garnishing if desired, and toss gently. Cover and chill 8 to 24 hours. Garnish with parsley sprigs.

MAKES 8 SERVINGS

POTATOBURGERS

> *³/₄ pound ground beef*
> *³/₄ cup ground or grated Maine potatoes*
> *¹/₄ cup ground or grated onions*
> *2 tablespoons chopped green pepper*
> *1 teaspoon salt*
> *Drippings, fat, or oil*
> *1 cup tomato juice (or 1 eight-ounce can tomato sauce)*

1 *tablespoon flour*
2 *or* 3 *tablespoons water*

Mix together the ground beef, potatoes, onions, green pepper, and salt. When well combined, form into 4 or 5 flat cakes. Brown in the drippings, fat, or oil in a frying pan, turning once. Add the tomato juice or tomato sauce, lower the heat, cover, and simmer 25 minutes. Remove the potatoburgers from the frying pan and keep them hot. Combine the flour and water and stir it into the frying pan. Stir until thickened, and pour over the potatoburgers.

MAKES 4 OR 5 SERVINGS

POTATO YEAST ROLLS

2 *cups milk*
$^1/_2$ *cup cooked, mashed Maine potatoes*
$^1/_2$ *cup sugar*
$^1/_2$ *cup butter or margarine*
$^1/_2$ *teaspoon salt*
1 *package active dry yeast (or* 1 *yeast cake)*
$5^1/_2$ *to* 6 *cups flour*
$^1/_2$ *teaspoon baking soda*
1 *teaspoon baking powder*

In a saucepan mix together the milk, mashed potatoes, suger, butter or margarine, and salt. Heat to the boiling point, stirring constantly. Remove from the heat, pour into a bowl, and cool to lukewarm, about 115°. Dissolve the yeast in a small amount of the lukewarm mixture and allow to stand about 5 minutes in a warm place until foamy. Add to the potato mixture.

Sift together $5^1/_2$ cups of the flour, the baking soda, and the baking powder, and add to the first mixture. Mix well. Place in a greased bowl, cover, and let rise in a warm place 1 hour.

Turn out on a floured board. Knead in about $^1/_2$ cup more flour to make a firm dough. Knead until smooth. If you wish to use the dough at once, let it rise again in a warm place, covered, until doubled in bulk. Knead lightly and shape into Parkerhouse, cloverleaf, or any desired shape rolls. (For Parkerhouse rolls, roll out with a rolling pin, cut into rounds with a biscuit cutter, make a depression across the center of the round with the handle of a dinner knife, fold over, and press the edges together lightly. Arrange in a greased baking pan. To make cloverleaf rolls, roll small balls of dough in the palms of the hands and arrange 3 of the balls in each depression of greased muffin tins.) Cover the rolls and set them in a warm place to rise until doubled in bulk.

Meanwhile, preheat the oven at 400°. Bake the rolls 15 to 20 minutes until nicely browned.

If you wish to store all or part of the dough, place it in a bowl, cover, and refrigerate. When ready to use it, knead it down, shape it into rolls, and let them rise in greased pans in a warm place for 1 to $1^1/_2$ hours, or until doubled in bulk, then bake as above.

MAKES ABOUT 3 DOZEN ROLLS

POTATO FUDGE

3 squares unsweetened baking chocolate
1 tablespoon butter
$^1/_3$ cup cooked, mashed Maine potatoes
$^1/_8$ teaspoon salt
1 teaspoon vanilla extract
3 to 4 cups confectioner's sugar, sifted

Melt the chocolate and butter in a double boiler over hot water. Add the mashed potatoes, salt, and vanilla extract, and mix well. Add the confectioner's sugar a little at a time, mixing well, until the mixture will not absorb any more sugar. Turn out onto a board. Knead until smooth. Press into a buttered 8-inch-square pan. Cut into squares.

MAKES 16 PIECES

VARIATION: Press a walnut half onto each fudge square.

Festival Facts

The Houlton Potato Feast, which began in 1957, is held for one day annually in early July in Houlton, Maine, which is at the intersection of U.S. 1 and Interstate 95 in the northeastern part of the state. For additional information, write: Houlton Chamber of Commerce, 109 Main Street, Houlton, Maine 04730.

The Maine Potato Blossom Festival, which began in 1948, is held annually for four days in mid-July in Fort Fairfield, Maine, which is about forty-five miles north of Houlton on Alternate U.S. 1. For further information, write: Fort Fairfield Chamber of Commerce, Fort Fairfield, Maine 04742.

Pumpkin Show

29

Circleville, Ohio

Pie in the face is not usually an appealing idea, but if you happen to be in the middle of the Pumpkin Pie Eating Contest at the Pumpkin Show in Circleville, Ohio, it's not only appealing but practical to get on intimate terms with a pie to avoid the time-consuming use of a fork. A pie-eating contest is a marvelous way for pumpkin-pie lovers to satisfy their craving for the autumnal treat in a gluttonous and unmannerly way with the complete approval of society. A less messy way to enjoy pumpkin pie, of which hundreds are made and sold at the Pumpkin Show, is to buy a slice at one of the booths set up in the festival area.

Ten blocks in Circleville are closed off to traffic at festival time, and within this area stages, games, and food booths are set up, with the latter serving a variety of pumpkin specialties wide enough to send a pumpkin fancier into ecstasy. One can have a delicious pumpkinburger (somewhat on the order of a Sloppy Joe) to start off the sampling tour, move on to a booth selling pumpkin soup, taste the gently seasoned wares of the pumpkin pancake people, carry on with a taste of creamy pumpkin ice cream, and finish off with a stop at a candy booth for some enticing pumpkin fudge. In between, there's a choice of pumpkin doughnuts, pumpkin breads galore, pumpkin waffles, pumpkin milk shakes and sundaes (including pumpkin fudge sundaes), pumpkin cookies of all kinds, pumpkin brittle, and pumpkin taffy.

To emphasize the local admiration of pumpkin pie, Lindsey's Bake Shop in Circleville bakes a 5-foot-diameter, 370-pound version of the dessert each year for the Pumpkin Show, and Miss Pumpkin, queen of the festival, joyously poses holding a slice of pie that weighs somewhere around 23 pounds.

Other pumpkin aficionados hasten to enter the Bake A Pumpkin Pie Contest, where awards are offered for the Grand Champion Pumpkin Pie and the Champion Pumpkin Pie, and runner-up prizes are given for third- and fourth-place pumpkin pies. Not *everyone* confines pumpkin-contest cooking to pies, however, and there are cake, bread, cookie, and candy categories in the many baked-goods contests taking place.

The Pumpkin Show, which is Ohio's oldest festival, is also the sixth largest festival in the United States, and has enjoyed calling itself the Greatest Free Show in the World since 1903. At that time the town's Mayor Haswell decided to decorate the front of his place of business on Circleville's West Main Street with some of the profusion of locally grown pumpkins and bundles of corn shocks. He asked farmers to bring in specimens of the biggest pumpkins they had grown and to exhibit them in an area set aside on the then-unpaved street, called in the Yellowbud Band to lead a parade around town, and invited one and all to pull on their best boots or tie on their prettiest bonnets and get together to compare notes on corn and pumpkin crops, compete for the largest pumpkin grown, promenade, socialize, and see whatever sights there were in Circleville.

The next year, other merchants followed the idea of dressing the town for fall and draped their storefronts in bunting, put out bunches of corn shocks, and piled up pumpkins, many carved into smiling or grimacing jack-o'-lanterns, to give the whole street a festive harvest appearance. Pumpkin-pie-baking contests were added to what had already become a festival, as were other activities and contests through the years, until today they include a Miss Pumpkin Show, a Little Miss Pumpkin Show, a parade for pets, another for babies, another for bands, and yet another for the queen, a home arts and crafts show featuring quilts, afghans, articles for the home, clothing, accessories, and crafts made by local people, an art show featuring the work of area artists, a flower show, baked and canned goods contests, and a fruit and vegetable show where all varieties, shapes, and sizes of produce are exhibited.

But of all these events the oldest and still the most impressive is the Annual Pumpkin Weigh-Off, which challenges anyone, and particularly the commercial pumpkin-growing community of Half Moon Bay, California, to beat the world's record-sized pumpkin grown in Circleville in 1975 by George and Mark Coon. Their pumpkin, classified as a Hungarian Gray, weighed a staggering 378 pounds and won its growers first-prize money plus a dollar for every pound of its weight over 250 pounds.

By tradition the giant-sized winning pumpkin is sold on the last day of the show to a supermarket owner in Parkersburg, West Virginia, who displays it until the week before Thanksgiving, when it is delivered to a local bakery that makes it into as many as 320 pumpkin pies which are donated to the Salvation Army. The seeds of the pumpkin, considered to be the property of its grower, are thoughtfully sent back to Circleville before the pies go into the oven.

Along with the pumpkin weigh-off there are also other competitions among growers for the largest of several varieties of pumpkins with names like Tan-Cheese, Red Cow, or just plain Best Pie Pumpkin. Gourds, inedible cousins of the pumpkin, are given prizes for the best Turks Turbans, Crown of Thorns, Warties, Spoons, and Freaks. Everywhere there are displays of pumpkins of all kinds, in stacks and in rows, the heaviest of them having been moved to their locations on canvas tarps, with four to six men lifting them into place where they remain until the festival's end. Some of the pumpkins are cut into jack-o'-lanterns or expertly carved. Bob Spohn of Columbus, Ohio, for example, makes a unique pumpkin exhibit for the show each year by carving pumpkins into three-dimensional faces or other shapes and adding paint and accessories to complete his seasonal works of art.

In all, there are over a hundred thousand pounds of pumpkins and gourds on display. More pumpkins appear in the parades, where, for instance, a float might be made up of a tremendous artificial pumpkin-shell coach wherein sits Cinderella on her way to the ball. Pumpkins in other floats are gilded or otherwise dressed up to stand out in the parade.

If one cares to get away from pumpkins for just a moment, there are other things to do. One can listen to the uninhibited souls who enter the Hog-Calling Contest, watch the Egg-Tossing Contest, see baton twirlers and stage shows, or hear concerts provided for entertainment.

Back in the early days, Circleville (which, incidentally, was originally laid out in a circle with streets radiating out from a hexagonally shaped courthouse in its center) was in the center of a commercial pumpkin-growing area, and pumpkins were then grown to be sold to local canneries. Nowadays, the pumpkins are simply marketed for Halloween jack-o'-lanterns and home cooking use as well as for display in fall arrangements and for festival use. People in Circleville know that the pumpkin, a true native American food plant, was a staple of many Indian tribes who introduced it to early settlers, and that pumpkin was served at the Pilgrims' first Thanksgiving dinner. While they like apples very much, Circleville folk remind you that apples were imported into America from Europe, and so these people are very much in favor of changing the well-known phrase to "as American as pumpkin pie." It's food for thought.

The recipes below are for Pumpkinburgers (provided by the Crusader Sunday School Class of the Calvary United Methodist Church of Circleville), Pumpkin Pancakes (provided by the Kiwanis Club of Circleville), Pumpkin Ice Cream, and Old-fashioned Pumpkin Fudge.

PUMPKINBURGERS

1 *medium onion, chopped*
1¹/₂ *pounds ground beef*
1 *twelve-ounce jar chili sauce*
¹/₂ *cup mashed pumpkin (canned or freshly made)*
1 *teaspoon salt*
Pepper to taste
1 *teaspoon pumpkin-pie spice*
1 *can tomato soup*
Hamburger buns

Combine the onions and ground beef, and sauté in a skillet until the meat loses its color. Add the remaining ingredients (except the hamburger buns) and mix well, cover, and simmer over low heat about 1 hour. Serve on hamburger buns.

MAKES ABOUT 8 SERVINGS

PUMPKIN PANCAKES

2 *cups biscuit mix (such as Bisquick)*
¹/₂ *teaspoon cinnamon*
1 *cup milk*
1 *egg*
¹/₂ *cup mashed pumpkin (canned or freshly made)*

Combine the biscuit mix and cinnamon. Add the milk, egg, and pumpkin, and mix until blended. Drop onto a hot, oiled griddle, spreading out each pancake with the back of a spoon, and bake until bubbles appear on top. Turn and brown the other side. Serve with butter and syrup as desired.

MAKES 1 DOZEN

PUMPKIN ICE CREAM

$^1/_4$ *cup brown sugar*
$^1/_8$ *teaspoon salt*
$^1/_2$ *teaspoon cinnamon*
$^1/_4$ *teaspoon ginger*
$^1/_4$ *cup milk*
$^1/_2$ *teaspoon vanilla extract*
$^1/_2$ *cup mashed pumpkin (canned or freshly made)*
1 *cup heavy cream*

Combine the brown sugar, salt, cinnamon, and ginger. Add the milk, vanilla extract, and pumpkin, and mix well. Whip the cream until stiff. Add a spoonful or two of the pumpkin mixture, and stir until combined. Add the whipped-cream mixture to the pumpkin mixture, and fold in gently but thoroughly. Turn into a shallow pan and freeze until partially frozen. Empty into a bowl, break up, and beat well with an electric mixer. Pack into a 1-quart plastic container, cover, and freeze until firm.

MAKES ABOUT 4 SERVINGS

OLD-FASHIONED PUMPKIN FUDGE

2 *cups sugar*
2 *tablespoons light corn syrup*
1 *tablespoon mashed pumpkin (canned or freshly made)*
Pinch of salt
$^1/_4$ *teaspoon pumpkin-pie spice*
$^1/_3$ *cup milk*
$^1/_3$ *cup sweetened condensed milk*
2 *tablespoons butter*
$^1/_2$ *teaspoon vanilla extract*
2 *drops orange food coloring (optional)*

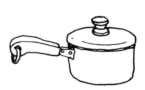

In a saucepan combine the sugar, corn syrup, pumpkin, salt, pumpkin-pie spice, milk, and condensed milk. Place over medium-high heat and cook, stirring constantly, until the mixture comes to a boil. Reduce the heat and cook, stirring occasionally, until the mixture reaches the soft-ball stage (238°). Remove from the heat and allow to cool until still slightly hot. Add the butter and stir until melted. Add the vanilla extract and food coloring if desired. (The fudge is a pretty natural pumpkin color without it.) Beat with a spoon until the mixture is very thick, creamy, and begins to hold its shape and lose its shine. Pour into a baking pan or refrigerator tray (about 5x9 inches) which has been lined with buttered aluminum foil. Smooth the top of the fudge and allow it to set until cool and firm. Cut into squares.

MAKES ABOUT 1¼ POUNDS, OR 27 PIECES

Festival Facts

The Circleville Pumpkin Show, which began in 1903, is held annually for four days starting on the third Wednesday of October in Circleville, Ohio, which is at the intersection of U.S. 22 and 23, about twenty-five miles south of Columbus. For further information, write: Circleville Pumpkin Show, Inc., P.O. Box 228, Circleville, Ohio 43113.

International Rice Festival

30

Crowley, Louisiana

According to an old Chinese myth, a handful of rice was once thrown into a well belonging to a poor but unselfish woman, and it turned the water into an endless supply of wine, making the old woman quite rich and allowing her to live happily ever after. Rice doesn't cause water to turn into wine in Louisiana, unless, of course, a chance Japanese visitor should decide to brew a barrel of sake, but it has provided very prosperous livelihoods for many people and has become a large part of the state's economic picture. It follows that lots of people are living happily ever after in Acadia Parish (county) in southwest Louisiana, where the rice grows tall, full, and abundantly.

Each year after the rice has been harvested and before the soybeans, grown as an additional crop by many rice farmers, are ready to be harvested, there's time for the farmers, the millers, and everyone concerned with the rice industry to take time out to celebrate the rice harvest in Crowley, which has come to be known as the Rice Capital of America.

At a prefestival banquet the Rice Farmer of the Year and his younger counterpart, the Junior Rice Farmer of the Year, are honored for their contributions to agriculture in general but especially to rice agriculture through their farming activities and work with agricultural organizations at levels ranging from the 4-H Club for the Junior Rice Farmer to membership on the board of a soil conservation group or appointment to the Louisiana Rice Research Board for the Rice Farmer. Honors are given, too, before the festival for rice grading. Nine different varieties of rice are grown in the area, with medium-grain and long-grain leading the way, and awards are given for rice grading, the grain being judged for its beauty, fullness, and quantity yield.

On opening day, festival visitors get into direct contact with rice. One way a Cajun (a corruption of the word *Acadian*) shows his love for rice at the affair is to enter the Rice-Eating Contest, apparently the only such event of its kind held in the state, and to gobble down as many plateful of the fluffy white grains as he can before the clock runs out. Everyone from schoolboy to senator has been known to enter, and the winner is presented, quite fittingly, with a silver spoon so he can be assured of eating all future rice in style.

Those who view rice as the queen of cuisine prefer to do marvelous things with it before they sit down to the table, and this group of Cajun cooks enters the Creole Rice-Cooking Contest armed with treasured recipes for favorite local dishes. While anyone, regardless of place of residence, can enter the contest, most contestants are from southwest Louisiana or Texas. Each dish they enter must contain rice or rice by-products, which would include, for example, rice cereals or brands of beer which contain rice. (Budweiser beer is brewed with rice, and its makers are the largest commercial purchasers of the United States rice crop. Their famous Clydesdale horses are exhibited at the Rice Festival where the livestock show is held.)

There are three main divisions of the contest, Rice and Meat, Rice and Seafood, and Rice Desserts, with a Men's, Women's, and Junior Cook's Contest held in each division, with the exception of the Dessert Division, which doesn't seem to attract male cooks. A score or more of hostesses assist at the contest by looking after the guests, answering questions, and so on. Judges in each division sample such creole delicacies as homemade boudin (sausages made from pork steaks, heart, liver, and kidney, hog heads, rice, red pepper, onion, and garlic); creole rice with meat and cabbage; rice, soybean, and meat pie; stuffed creole rice bread; fisherman's dish (containing red fish, frogs' legs, shrimp, crawfish, crabmeat, and oysters); okra, rice, and shrimp; and stuffed frogs' legs.

Three outstanding dishes that recently won prizes at the contest are given below and include Baked Cornish Hens with Creole Rice Dressing entered in the Women's Rice and Meat Division by Mrs. Ben Daigle of Church Point, Louisiana, Eggplant Rice Dressing entered in the Junior Rice and Meat Division by Anthony Dartez of Kaplan, Louisiana, and Rice and Crab Salad entered in the Junior Rice and Seafood division by Chelsa Lormand of Ville Platte, Louisiana.

Although teenage Anthony Dartez's family is not in the rice business, they are all enthusiastic rice eaters, and Anthony's recipe is one they often have at home with barbecued meat, a roast, or baked chicken. A 4-H member who enjoys cooking, Anthony likes rice so much that he feels his meal isn't complete without it.

Chelsa Lormand is also an ardent rice devotee. While her prizewinning crabmeat dish is reserved for special occasions, crabmeat costing what it does, every meal in her home includes a rice dish of some kind. Although she has named her dish Rice and Crab Salad because it is put into shells and can be eaten cold as well as hot, it is really most tempting served as a hot dish for a first course or main dish. Chelsa's family farms, and their principal crop is yams, so while she has so far won only one prize in rice cooking, she has won several in yam cooking, as well as another in egg cookery, and likes to cook for fun as well as to promote the agricultural products of her area.

One notices that any number of dressing recipes are entered

in the contest since Cajuns dote on the dish (sometimes called "dirty rice"), which they use for stuffing poultry, seafood, or anything else that takes their fancy, or bake and serve as a main dish since it contains a good deal of meat. Other things about Cajun cooking, as super prizewinner Mrs. Ben Daigle points out, are that recipes often call for more red pepper than most other cooks would use, and that many start off with a roux, which is a cooked mixture of oil and flour that imparts a special dark-brown roasted flavor to dishes and is the foundation of many sauces and gravies.

Mrs. Daigle, whose grandparents moved to the then new rice-growing area of Cajun country in southern Louisiana around the turn of the century, lived on a rice farm in her youth and married a man who was as involved with rice as she has always been. He sold oil for use in pumps needed to water rice, sold and serviced rice-farming equipment, and owned rice and feed mills. The Daigles also had large-acreage rice farms, belonged to the Rice Council for the marketing of rice, and attended many rice millers' conventions where they associated with people in all phases of the rice industry. Mrs. Daigle, now widowed, has been interested in rice cookery for years, and has what is probably a record-breaking collection of over ninety awards won for her entries in the Creole Rice-Cooking Contest over about the past thirty years. One of her great joys is sharing her recipes, food, and rice enthusiasm. She has encouraged her grandchildren, Posie, Laura, and Kevin Pool, to enter the contests, where they've all won ribbons, and when she visits relatives up North, she always carries along a few packages of her rice dressing (frozen) on the plane.

Cajuns like to dance almost as much as they like to eat rice dishes—provided, of course, it's dancing to French music. That's what's provided at a fais-do-do, a traditional dance in the area and an annual event at the Rice Festival. *Fais-do-do* means "go to sleep," and the peculiar name for the dance began years ago when farm couples would bring their children along to the dances, bundle them into bed in a room set aside for the purpose, and tell them to "fais-do-do" while they proceeded to dance the night away. The fais-do-do at the festival is a lively street dance with French songs and music that everyone dances to, free-style.

There are some goofy goings-on at the festival, which include a frog derby where granddaddy-sized frogs are urged on with the gentle nudging of sticks by their pretty girl "jockeys," a tricycle relay race for men over twenty-two years of age who have a hard time keeping out of the way of their own knees as they pedal along, a greased-pig contest, and a rope tug-of-war which can land the unlucky losers in a most uninviting mud puddle.

The Rice Festival goes the usual queen contest one better by having not only a Rice Festival Queen who knows how to cook rice and has, on occasion, won a prize for it, and a children's edition of Rice King and Queen, but also a Senior Citizen Rice Queen whose attendants are quite often her grandchildren. Children have a special parade all their own, made up of floats which they construct at their schools, following the theme of the year, and every float is decorated with bundles of gracefully waving rice cut at nearby farms.

Rice, in fact, is the main decoration of the festival. The grand parade is decked out with it, and it brightens up windows all around town. A window-decorating contest is held, with prizes awarded for the windows where rice is used with the most originality, in the greatest quantity, and in the most varied form. There's an annual theme for the windows, too, and rice is utilized in the plant with the rice still in the hulls, tinted different shades with food coloring, stacked up, poured out, and shown in every conceivable way by people who view rice as the single most important food in their lives, if not in a major part of the world. Agronomists would agree.

BAKED CORNISH HENS WITH CREOLE RICE DRESSING

FOR THE ROUX:

¹/₄ cup oil
¹/₂ cup flour

FOR THE DRESSING AND BIRDS:

1¹/₂ pounds ground, uncooked pork
1 pound ground, uncooked beef
1 pound uncooked chicken gizzards, trimmed and finely chopped or ground
¹/₂ pound uncooked chicken livers, trimmed and finely chopped or ground
1 cup chopped celery
¹/₂ cup chopped bell peppers
¹/₂ cup chopped onion
2 teaspoons salt (or to taste)
¹/₂ teaspoon black pepper (or to taste)
¹/₂ teaspoon cayenne pepper (or to taste)
¹/₂ cup oil
2 cups water
1 cup raw rice
2 tablespoons chopped green onion (scallion) tops (or to taste)
2 tablespoons chopped parsley (or to taste)
8 Rock Cornish hens*
Melted butter
Parsley, crabapples, or other garnishes (optional)

FOR THE ROUX: Heat the oil slightly in a heavy saucepan over medium heat, and stir in the flour. Cook over medium to low heat, stirring constantly, until the mixture becomes a dark golden brown. Do not allow to burn. Remove from the heat and set aside, stirring again if the oil begins to separate.

---

*This recipe will stuff from 4 to 10 or 12 hens, and you may use as many hens as you wish, spooning extra dressing around them in the pan, or you may omit the hens entirely and bake and serve the dressing as a main dish. The dressing may also be used to stuff duckling or other poultry.

FOR THE DRESSING AND BIRDS: Combine the pork, beef, chicken gizzards, chicken livers, celery, bell peppers, onion, salt, black pepper, cayenne pepper, and 1 tablespoon of the roux. (Store the balance of the roux in a glass jar in the refrigerator for use in sauces or other dishes.) Cook the meat-and-vegetable mixture in a large skillet in the $^1/_2$ cup oil until the meat is brown, turning frequently. Add the water and simmer gently about 30 minutes.

Meanwhile, cook the rice, covered, in a heavy saucepan in boiling water to cover by 1 inch. When the rice is cooked, add the green onion tops and parsley to the meat mixture and cook 2 minutes. Then add the cooked rice and mix well.

Preheat the oven at 325°. Stuff the hens with the dressing and arrange in a large baking pan. Spoon the remaining dressing around the birds. Bake 1 hour, or until the hens test done when a fork is inserted in the thigh, basting once or twice during the baking with melted butter so they brown nicely. Arrange the birds on a platter and spoon extra dressing around them. If desired, decorate with parsley, crabapples, or any desired garnish.

MAKES 8 SERVINGS

EGGPLANT RICE DRESSING

2 tablespoons salad oil
1 large onion, chopped
1 large green bell pepper, chopped
$^1/_4$ cup chopped green onion (scallion) tops
1 rib celery, chopped
$^1/_2$ pound ground beef or other meat*
1 medium eggplant, peeled and diced
$^1/_2$ cup raw rice
1 small hot pepper, stem and seeds removed
$1^1/_4$ cups water
Salt and pepper to taste

---

*Shrimp may be substituted for ground meat.

Heat the oil slightly and add the onion, green pepper, green onion tops, and celery. Sauté until the vegetables are soft. Add the ground meat and cook until lightly browned. Add the eggplant, rice, hot pepper, water, salt, and pepper. Reduce the heat, cover, and simmer, stirring often, 30 or 40 minutes, or until rice is done.

MAKES 6 OR MORE SERVINGS

RICE AND CRAB SALAD
(Rice and Crab in Shells—A Main Dish or Hot Appetizer)

1 cup cooked rice
1^1/$_2$ cups canned or fresh crabmeat, flaked
1 cup cream
6 hard-cooked eggs, chopped
1^1/$_2$ teaspoons chopped parsley
1 teaspoon minced onion
^{1}/$_2$ teaspoon salt
^{1}/$_4$ teaspoon cayenne pepper (or to taste)
^{1}/$_4$ teaspoon black pepper (or to taste)
^{1}/$_2$ cup grated American (or Cheddar) cheese

Preheat the oven at 350°. Combine all the ingredients except the grated cheese. Spoon into buttered shells, using 6 shells if it will be used for a main dish, or 8 to 10 small shells if it will be an appetizer. Sprinkle with the grated cheese. Bake about 20 minutes. (May also be served cold if desired.)

MAKES 6 TO 10 SERVINGS

Festival Facts

The International Rice Festival which began in 1937, is held annually for two days in mid-October in Crowley, which is on Route 13, about one mile south of Interstate 10 in southwestern Louisiana. For further information, write: International Rice Festival, P.O. Box 1444, Crowley, Louisiana 70526.

Ohio Swiss Festival

31

Sugarcreek, Ohio

Any woman who's ever felt like picking up a 75-pound rock and hurling it through the air without having her sanity or intent questioned has a chance to make her urge a reality at the Stein-stossen (stone-tossing) event held several times daily during the Ohio Swiss Festival. The unusual Swiss sport, a leading attraction at festivals in its native land, is apparently unpracticed anywhere in the United States except Sugarcreek. It has both a Men's and a Women's Division, with the weight of the men's stone about twice that of the ladies', and bringing the winner twice as much in prize money. The largest stone used anywhere is the Unspunnen stone in Switzerland, which weighs in at 183 pounds, about 45 pounds heavier than the men's stone used in

Sugarcreek's competition. You don't have to swing a stone, but only your opponent, in another Swiss athletic event at the festival. It's called Schwingfest, which translates to "Swiss wrestling," and exhibitions are given each afternoon.

Whether or not you've participated in either of these taxing sports, you'll probably want to have a snack of Swiss food before long. Swiss cheese sandwiches lead the way, since Sugarcreek is the center of the state's Swiss cheese industry and has more than twenty plants in the vicinity supplying tons of cheese to the festival annually. As one might guess, the early settlers of the area were Swiss farmers who learned the art of cheesemaking in their native canton, Bern. For those who want to have their cheese and eat it, too, Swiss cheese is also sold by the piece for taking home, as well as in the sandwiches. Swiss cookies (Schenckeli), apple fritters, Swiss pretzels (Bratzeli), Swiss cheese pie, fried cheese, trail bologna, and other foods can be bought for stand-up eating, and sit-down chicken dinners are served cafeteria-style at the Sugarcreek Fire Station. Recipes for Schenckeli, as prepared by the women of Sugarcreek's United Church of Christ for the festival, and for Swiss Cheese Pie are included below.

All the buildings in the downtown business section of Sugarcreek are built in Alpine design. After the town's first Swiss Festival was held, a local artist, Tom Miller, conceived the idea of buying one of the downtown buildings and remodeling it into a Swiss-type structure. The idea caught on, and the area has now taken on the appearance of a Swiss village, making it an all-year-round tourist attraction as well as a perfect background for the Swiss Festival.

Not only the buildings but many of the people look authentically Swiss, too. Residents as well as people from other parts of Ohio and out-of-staters arrive in Swiss outfits to compete for one of the many costume awards. They're given for the largest family all in costume, the oldest family, the youngest persons, and for those who have come the greatest distance in Swiss garb. Entertainers, too, wear the clothing of their ancestral land and lend a gay atmosphere to the festival with their yodeling and accordian music. Yodeling fans can buy records of professional yodelers which are available at the festival, and amateur yodelers can join a yodeling contest if they feel so inclined. The purpose of the contest is to encourage people to learn yodeling, since, unlike Swiss-cheese making, it seems in slight danger of becoming a lost art.

SCHENCKELI

1/2 cup butter
1 1/2 cups sugar
4 eggs
2 to 3 teaspoons grated lemon rind
1 teaspoon lemon extract
4 to 5 cups flour
1/2 teaspoon salt
1 teaspoon cream of tartar
1/2 teaspoon baking soda
Fat or oil for frying

Cream the butter until soft, gradually adding the sugar, and cream until fluffy. Add the eggs, one at a time, mixing well. Add the lemon rind and lemon extract. Sift together 4 cups of flour, the salt, cream of tartar, and baking soda, and gradually add to the dough. Add enough more flour to make a stiff dough. Cover and refrigerate 8 hours or overnight.

Roll out the dough 3/8-inch thick on a floured board and cut into strips 1/2- to 3/4-inch wide and about 3 inches long. Heat the fat or oil to 350° or 360° in a deep fryer or wok, and fry the strips, several at a time, until nicely browned, turning once. Drain on paper towels.

MAKES ABOUT 150

SWISS CHEESE PIE

1 nine- or ten-inch unbaked pie shell
3 eggs
2 cups milk
1 teaspoon salt
Dash of pepper
1/2 pound Swiss cheese, grated or shredded

Chill the unbaked pie shell thoroughly in the refrigerator or freezer. Preheat the oven at 400°. Beat the eggs and add the milk, salt, and pepper.

Sprinkle the cheese into the chilled pie shell. Pour the egg-milk mixture over the cheese. Bake 10 minutes. Reduce the oven heat to 350° and bake about 25 minutes longer, or until the pie is puffed, well browned, and a knife inserted in the center comes out clean. Serve hot.

MAKES 6 OR MORE SERVINGS

Festival Facts

The Ohio Swiss Festival, which began in 1953, is held annually on a Friday and Saturday in early October at Sugarcreek, Ohio, which is on Route 39, about ten miles from Dover, off Interstate 77. For further information, write: Secretary, Ohio Swiss Festival, Inc., c/o Chamber of Commerce, Sugarcreek, Ohio 44681.

Round Hill Highland Scottish Games

32

Stamford, Connecticut

The skirling of bagpipes, the beating of drums, and the flinging steps of Highland dancers each year lure thirteen to fourteen thousand people, not counting the children, to the estate of R. Colhoun in Stamford, Connecticut, where the Round Hill Highland Scottish Games are held. The pageantry, the tradition of competition in sports, and the almost instinctive urge of Scots to gather produces one of the most robust, clean, colorful, and earthy fairs one could hope to attend.

The gathering of the clans, another name for the Highland

games, is a centuries-old tradition brought from Scotland generations ago by early settlers, with the first games in the United States dating back to the days of the Revolution. There are now more than twenty-two million people of Scottish extraction in the United States, and among the gatherings they hold in various parts of the country yearly, the Round Hill Highland Games are unique in that they have the longest record of consecutive meetings anywhere. Their first meeting in 1923 was a picnic for Scottish immigrants, and they're now somewhere in the neighborhood of celebrating their fifty-first anniversary. To present Scottish music and traditions and to perpetuate the culture which the emigrating people of Scotland took with them not only to the United States but to Canada, Australia, and many other corners of the world as well, is the sole aim of the Round Hill Games, and all proceeds from the event are donated to a well-rounded group of charitable causes.

The exact origin of Highland games is lost somewhere in history, but probably the most accepted story is that a Scottish king in the eleventh century, seeking the fastest available runner to act as his courier, held a foot-race competition that started off on level ground but ended up at the peak of a craggy mountain, thus testing the strength and endurance of the contestants. This became the first Highland game, and the attraction for similar rugged sports for Scotsmen has lasted through generations, showing no sign of slackening. Not only a variety of track events, soccer, and other team sports, but hurdle jumping, the shot put, the hammer toss, and the caber toss are all popular and traditional at the Highland games.

Most spectacular of all these male-strength-proving sports is the caber toss, a feat of daring, strength, balance, and coordination unheard of outside Scottish sports. The caber itself is a tall fir tree stripped of its branches and very much resembling a telephone pole in appearance and weight. The caber is held upright by game attendants and approached by the contestant, who must pick it up from the bottom, lift it, and keep it balanced while he runs forward, flings it into the air, and makes it flip over and land vertically on its opposite end. If all has gone well up to this point, the caber falls in the direction away from the contestant and ends horizontally in a direct line from the starting point.

The most eye-pleasing part of the Round Hills Highland Games is the dress of the people, who turn out in the kilts and plaids (shawl pieces) of their tartans (patterns in the weave of the material, which are different for each clan) to view the proceedings in their quietly jovial way or to compete in the piping, drumming, and dancing competitions. Bits of heather are pinned to clothing, buckled shoes gleam in the sunlight, smart socks are held in place by bright tartan ribbons, and here and there a skean dhu, which is a small dagger, is fastened through the garterlike sock ribbon of some of the men, where it is held in place against the calf. Sometimes the old and new merge in amusing but acceptable ways of dress, as when one young man wearing an authentic kilt topped it off with a T-shirt emblazoned with "Kiss" in large black letters across the front.

Dancing, the most popular women's competition, is an exhausting art, with the Highland fling probably ranking as the most well-known dance, and the sword dance following a close second. The Highland fling, whose name comes from the flinging out of one leg first in front and then in back while the dancer continuously hops in place on the other foot, is executed with equal vigor by four-year-olds who enter the Baby Class Event, through the Adult Class of seventeen years and over. The seann tribhas and sailor's hornpipe are also much danced in the competition, and there is even, oddly, an Irish jig judged as the last dancing event of the day.

Highland dancing and piping prowess are assessed by top-ranking judges who maintain high standards obvious even to the non-Scot watching the competition. Both amateur and open piping and drumming events take place, and the pipers are judged on finger control, agility, and timing rather than on the ability to blow hard, since a bagpipe, despite all efforts by the player, is incapable of having its volume increased or decreased in any way. A pipe has a range of only nine notes and, once started, has no shutting-off device. Players of all ages, with a noticeable number of younger contestants, attest to the resurgence of interest in learning to play the bagpipes. Teachers of the instrument are said to be in short supply, and thus in great demand. While the pip-ing draws a goodly crowd, the Scots, being honest folk, will confess that although the bagpipe is always associated with Scot-land, not *all* Scots like to associate with bagpipes.

Drums played along with bagpipes are truly blood-stirring, and the highlight of the Round Hill Games is the massed bands that end the day's festivities with marching and playing in a diz-zying display of color and sound. Some of the eleven bands are dressed in military style, and others are formal, complete with velvet jackets, full cuffs, and silver buttons on their jackets. The piping bands are led by tall, splendidly attired drum majors wearing towering black feather bonnets, the kilts of the march-ing players swing back and forth, the air is filled with excite-ment, and the cameras click away to record a riot of color and vi-tality not to be missed.

But long before day's end, hungry Scots and visitors alike queue up to fortify themselves with traditional baked Scottish Pies or with another Scottish favorite, Fish and Chips. "No mat-ter what an Englishman may say," you will hear, "Fish and Chips are of Scottish origin."

Molds for making Scottish Pies are imported from Scotland, and the pies are produced in mass proportions for the Round Hill Games. To duplicate the process would be unworkable in the home, but Mr. Reginald Cunningham, an official of the Round Hill Games, has donated the recipe which he brought with him from Scotland, where he baked Scottish Pies many years ago. His recipe has been adapted to making an American family-sized yield, but the principles remain the same. The shells for the pies are made several days ahead, since they need time to dry out before baking in order to be filled and baked without the support of pie pans. Filling for the pies in Scotland would be made of ground mutton or lamb, but at the Highland games, as in most places in America where Scottish Pies are made, ground beef is used instead.

The recipe here for Fish and Chips has also been adapted to home production from the commercially produced dish served at the games.

People who don't choose to buy their Scottish Pies or Fish and Chips at the games either bring their own or other simple, basic foods typical of the Scots. They eat them at appetizing and orderly picnics under shady trees throughout the grounds. A Scottish specialty often brought from home for a picnic sweet is Scottish Shortbread, and Mr. Cunningham has also provided us with his recipe for that traditional treat. Beer quenches the parched throats of the field and track contestants, a bit of Scotch sustains a few sturdy souls, and soft drinks are available at the games, but in general one would be well advised to bring along a jug of some cooling drink to ward off the thirsts engendered by a warm summer's day and the liveliness of the Round Hill Highland Games.

SCOTTISH PIES

FOR THE PASTRY:
  $1/4$ to $1/3$ pound beef suet
  2 tablespoons margarine
  2 teaspoons salt
  7 tablespoons water
  1 cup cake flour
  3 cups all-purpose flour

FOR THE FILLING:
  1 cup soft bread crumbs
  1 teaspoon salt
  Pepper to taste
  Water
  2 or 3 tablespoons finely chopped or grated onion
  1 pound ground beef or mutton

FOR THE PASTRY: Melt enough beef suet, finely cut, over a low flame, to measure 7 tablespoons. Add the margarine, and heat until melted. Dissolve the salt in the water and set aside. Pour the melted fat and margarine into a bowl and add the flour, mixing with a spoon—and later with the fingers if necessary—until crumbly and well combined. Make a hole in the center and pour in the salted water. Draw the flour mixture into the water and combine well. Roll out two-thirds of the mixture on a floured board and cut 10 to 12 circles $4^1/_4$ inches in diameter, using a cardboard pattern for a guide. Mold each circle over the *back* protrusions of standard-size muffin tins (ungreased) to form deep tart shells. Roll out the balance of the pastry as thinly as possible and cut 10 to 12 circles $3^1/_2$ inches in diameter, which will be used as tops for the pies. Cut a small hole in the center of each circle. Place the circles on ungreased baking sheets. Set all aside in a cool, dry place where they will be undisturbed for 24 hours. Carefully lift off the shells from the muffin tins and set them upright on an ungreased baking sheet. Allow all pastry to remain another 24 hours or longer if desired.

When ready to prepare the pies, preheat the oven at 400°.

FOR THE FILLING: Combine the bread crumbs, salt, pepper, and enough water to just moisten the crumbs. Mix in the onion. Add the ground meat and combine well. Place the shells on a baking sheet and fill three-fourths full with the meat mixture. Place the tops over the pies. Bake 30 minutes.

MAKES 10 TO 12 PIES

FISH AND CHIPS

> $1^1/_4$ to $1^1/_2$ pounds haddock or similar white fish
> 1 cup biscuit mix (such as Bisquick)
> 1 teaspoon baking powder
> $^1/_4$ teaspoon salt
> $^2/_3$ cup milk
> 4 baking potatoes*
> Vegetable oil
> Flour

Peel the potatoes and cut into strips $^1/_2$-inch thick and $^1/_2$-inch wide. Dry thoroughly on paper towels.

---

*Two packages of frozen French-fried potatoes may be substituted. Prepare according to the package directions.

Cut the haddock into serving pieces and dry thoroughly on paper towels. Combine the biscuit mix, baking powder, and salt. Add the milk and beat well with an egg beater.

Heat 4 to 5 inches of vegetable oil in a deep-fat fryer or 2 to 3 inches in a wok to a temperature of 375°. Fry the potatoes in several batches until crisp and browned. Drain on paper towels and keep warm while preparing the fish.

Lower the heat of the vegetable oil to 350°. Dip the haddock pieces first in the flour on both sides, then in the batter on both sides, and fry a few pieces at a time, turning once, until nicely browned. Drain on paper towels. Serve with the chips.

MAKES 4 SERVINGS

SCOTTISH SHORTBREAD

$^1/_2$ *cup butter*
$^1/_2$ *cup margarine*
$^1/_2$ *cup sugar*
4 *cups flour*

Preheat the oven at 375°. Cream the butter and margarine together until soft and well blended. Blend in the sugar. Add the flour gradually until the dough is hard to mix with a spoon. Turn the dough out on a board and blend in the remaining flour by rubbing it in with the heel of the hand. Pat it out in small rounds, crimping the edges with the fingers, or pat into two pie pans. The shortbread should be about $^1/_2$-inch thick.

Prick all over lightly with the tines of a fork. Poke through once or twice with the point of a sharp knife for air holes. If using a pie pan, mark wedges with the back of a knife to use as guidelines for cutting wedges after baking. If baking rounds, arrange on an ungreased baking sheet. Bake 30 to 35 minutes. Test by cutting a small corner off one piece of the shortbread and seeing if it is done all the way through.

Remove from the oven. Cut wedges with a sharp knife immediately, but do not remove the shortbread from the pan. If desired, sprinkle with sugar. After 10 to 15 minutes, remove from the pan and place on a wire rack to finish cooling.

MAKES ABOUT 24 PIECES

Festival Facts

The Round Hill Highland Scottish Games, which began in 1923, are held every year on July 4 on the estate of R. Colhoun, Davenport Ridge Road, Stamford, Connecticut. It can be reached from the Merritt Parkway, Exit 35 and 36 via High Ridge Road. For further information, write: Round Hill Scottish Games Association, P.O. Box 271, Greenwich, Connecticut 06830.

Syttende Mai

33

Stoughton, Wisconsin

If you're a troll, as any lover of Norwegian folklore knows, you live in an underground cavern, are kind to people in spite of the fact that you enjoy stealing their provisions, can foretell the future, endow humans with fortunes or superhuman strength if you feel so inclined, and are probably quite ugly. Trolls apparently enjoy being something less than beautiful and make the most of it at the Syttende Mai celebration in Stoughton, Wisconsin, each year when the Ugliest Troll Contest is held. Schoolchildren, under the guidance of their school art departments, design and make their own terrible-looking troll heads in an effort to outdo each other in looking hideous.

Quite possibly, trolls would not be so uncomely if they

received a steady diet of Norwegian dishes and delicacies such as one can buy at the Syttende Mai celebration. The women prepare sumptuous smorgasbords, and there are snacks and other foods and specialties. Brats, or hot dogs, are served in a novel way, as they are sometimes in Norway, by substituting lefse for hot-dog rolls. Lefse are breads made from a potato-and-flour dough and baked on a special iron, then rolled around the hot dogs. The Covenant Lutheran Church or the Jaycees usually make this specialty for the event.

Other groups, such as the Sons of Norway, Christ Lutheran Church, and Rebekah's Norse Snacks, make a myriad of Norwegian delicacies, with the most interesting and out-of-the-ordinary foods leaning toward meat dishes, desserts, and pastry creations. Södt-suppe, a red fruit pudding, and römmegröt, a thickened cream mixture served with melted butter, cinnamon, and sugar, are two well-liked desserts to be sampled. One notices that special irons are used for making some Norwegian dishes in addition to lefse, and that a number of cookie recipes utilize them. Krum kager, for example, cookies popular at the festival, are baked on an iron and rolled into cone shapes, and rosettes are made from a simple dough fried with the aid of a rosette iron. Sandbakkelse are pretty almond cookies baked in little fluted patty tins. Not requiring special utensils are the well-known fattigmann, little fried, diamond-shaped pastries, and the equally good but richer and more unusual Berliner-kranser.

Norwegians make a number of pressed-meat dishes which are then thinly sliced and sometimes cooked again before serving, or are served cold at the smorgasbord. At Syttende Mai one can sample rulla pulsa (a rolled, pressed flank steak), kalvadans (a pressed-veal dish), pulsa (a molded beef-heart-and-barley dish which is sliced and fried), and blö-klub (a sort of blood pudding which is sliced and sautéed in butter and served with a little cream poured over it). Other meat dishes prepared by Stoughton women are sulta (pork which is placed in brine after, rather than before, cooking), dyresteg (venison or beef steak), spekekjot (mutton or beef placed in brine for two weeks, then smoked or hung until dried), and kalvefiled med sur flote (veal with sour cream).

More than a hundred thousand people gather annually to

enjoy the foods as well as the distinctive crafts, beautifully made costumes, folk dancing, music, plays, and other gala Norse entertainment at Syttende Mai. Syttende Mai, which means "May 17" in Norwegian, marks the anniversary of the Norwegian Declaration of Independence from Sweden in 1814. Although Stoughton was first settled by New Englanders, by 1900 so many people from Norway had arrived that they far outnumbered other residents, and the town became a "Little Norway" with its own Norwegian-language newspaper, church services held in Norwegian, children who learned their first words of English when they began attending schools in Stoughton, and emotional commemorations of Syttende Mai by people still closely linked to their native land. Stoughton still has the largest population of Norwegian extraction anywhere in the United States today, and the townspeople, both Norwegian and non-Norwegian alike, now enjoy celebrating Norwegian Independence Day together each year.

Norwegian folk art plays a large part in the three-day event, with rosemaling one of the more unusual arts demonstrated and exhibited. Literally translated as "rose painting," rosemaling is a 275-year-old peasant craft first practiced by people living in remote areas of Norway where long and harsh winters made such diversions an important part of indoor life. Boxes, trunks, plates, and other items are decorated in designs and colors that vary from district to district in Norway but, in general, share a common starting point of a baroque vine and flower design in greens, reds, yellows, whites, and some blue, against backgrounds of dull blues, blue-greens, dull reds, and red-orange. What makes one person's rosemaling better than another's is creative design, degree of technical proficiency, harmonious blendings of colors, accented areas, and brushstrokes. Exhibit ribbons are awarded in several classes, including one for beginners, during the Syttende Mai event.

Costumes, handsomely and authentically designed through careful research and communication with people in Norway who know the differences among the many regional, seasonal, everyday, and festive-occasion costumes, are another high point of the celebration. Some of the costumes are made at the town's costume-making course held during the year, and hours are spent on embroidery, appliqué, beadwork, trimming, and other detailing on the garments. The Norwegian Style Show that shows off each creation to its best advantage is an event not to be missed at Syttende Mai.

Another must is the Norwegian Dancers, a thoroughly trained high school group, who, in spite of a continually changing membership as the young people graduate and leave school, are skilled and talented enough to make annual tours and once to have danced a command performance before the king of Norway.

Plays about Norway, troll hunts, visits to the Stoughton Historical Museum, which contains memorabilia of the town's past, concerts of Norwegian music, citywide displays of Norwegian goods and artifacts, and more, make this festival a rewarding one to visit.

The recipes that follow are for Berliner-Kranser (provided by the Candy Stripers of Stoughton's Community Hospital, who have collected a number of the community's Syttende Mai recipes into a little booklet which they sell at the festival and elsewhere to aid their volunteer hospital work), Pulsa, and Kalvefiled med Sur Flote.

BERLINER-KRANSER

2 hard-cooked egg yolks
$3/4$ cup sugar
2 unbeaten egg yolks
$1/2$ teaspoon almond extract
$1/2$ pound butter, softened
3 cups sifted flour
2 eggs whites, slightly beaten with a fork
Coarse sugar

Break up the hard-cooked egg yolks with a fork, or put them through a sieve. Combine with the sugar. Add the unbeaten egg yolks and almond extract, and mix lightly. Add the softened butter and mix well with a wooden spoon. Add the flour and mix well, using the hands to blend in all the flour.

Preheat the oven at 350°. Pull off small pieces of the dough and roll them between the palms of the hands or on a board until the dough is about the thickness of a pencil. Form into wreaths about $2^1/4$ inches in diameter. Dip into the egg white and arrange on greased baking sheets. Sprinkle with coarse sugar. Bake about 12 minutes until lightly browned.

MAKES ABOUT $3^1/2$ DOZEN

PULSA
(Barley Sausage)

> 1 small beef heart
> 1 tablespoon salt
> Barley (generous $^1/2$ cup for each pound of beef heart)
> 2 cups chopped onions
> Fat or oil
> $^1/4$ cup molasses
> 1 tablespoon marjoram
> Pepper to taste

Cut the beef heart open, removing any tubes and fibers, or have the butcher do this for you. Score all over and soak in cold water to cover for 2 hours. Drain, place in a pot, and cover with boiling water. Add the salt, bring to a boil, and skim until particles no longer rise to the surface. Reduce the heat, cover partially, and simmer until tender, $1^1/2$ hours or longer, depending on the size of the beef heart.

Meanwhile, soak the barley in cold water to cover.

When the heart is tender, remove from the water and add the barley to water. Cook, adding boiling water if necessary, until tender.

When cool enough to handle, cut up the heart, removing any undesirable parts, and put through a meat grinder or food processor. Combine with the cooked barley and put through the grinder or food processor again.

Sauté the onions in the fat or oil until soft. Add them to the beef-barley mixture along with the molasses, marjoram, and pepper. Pack into a rectangular-shaped container. Cover and chill. Slice and sauté in fat or oil.

MAKES 20 SERVINGS OR MORE,
DEPENDING ON THE SIZE OF THE BEEF HEART

KALVEFILED MED SUR FLOTE
(Veal Scallops with Sour Cream)

> ¹/₂ cup finely chopped onion
> Butter
> Vegetable oil
> 6 veal scallops, pounded thin
> Salt to taste
> Pepper to taste
> 1 cup sour cream
> ¹/₂ cup shredded gjetost*

Sauté the onion in a small amount of butter and vegetable oil until soft. Remove the onions from the skillet. Pat the veal scallops dry with paper towels. Add a little more butter and vegetable oil to the skillet and brown the veal scallops, 2 or 3 at a time, turning once. Remove from the skillet. Sprinkle with salt and pepper. Return the onions to the skillet. Remove the skillet from the flame.

Add the sour cream and shredded gjetost and stir until blended. Cook over a low flame, stirring constantly, until the cheese has melted completely, but do not allow the mixture to boil. Return the veal scallops to the skillet and heat several minutes, basting the veal with the sauce.

MAKES 6 SERVINGS

---

*Gjetost is a Norwegian cheese, brown in color, slightly heavy in texture, and a little sweet in taste. It can be found in most stores that stock imported cheeses. It comes in a rectangular block and is usually wrapped in red or silver foil.

Festival Facts

Syttende Mai, which began in 1955 on an organized basis, is held for the three-day weekend nearest to May 17 annually in Stoughton, Wisconsin, which is on U.S. 51, about ten miles south of Madison. For further information, write: Syttende Mai Committee, Stoughton Chamber of Commerce, 143 West Main Street, Stoughton, Wisconsin 53589.

Texas State Arts and Crafts Fair

34

Kerrville, Texas

The antelope may have vanished, but the deer, turkeys, javelinas, and other wild creatures still play on the range around Kerrville, Texas, sometimes catching a glimpse of the nearby Guadalupe River as it winds its way through town on its journey to the Gulf of Mexico. Closer to town, cattle, sheep, and mohair-producing goats live on sprawling ranches. This is Texas hill country in the south-central part of the state, and in its midst is Kerrville, host to the annual Texas State Arts and Crafts Fair visited by about thirty thousand people yearly.

A newcomer, by some standards, to the fair world, the burgeoning Texas State Arts and Crafts Fair is in its sixth year (as of 1977) and still growing. Its growth now, however, is more in the form of refinement of quality than in the number of exhibitors and displays or the size of the fair altogether, and the exhibitions are limited to the work of about two hundred superior craftsmen and artists from all over Texas. What makes this crafts fair outstanding, besides the caliber of its exhibitors, is its inclusion of some out-of-the-ordinary foods available as refreshments.

Not content just to dole out hamburgers, hot dogs, and pizzas, it features local favorites such as chalupas, chili con queso, buñuelos, Mexican strip steak, and jalapeño fried chicken. For those who don't fancy Tex-Mex fare, there's a booth busy serving fried catfish, another selling turkey sausage, and still another selling a variety of natural foods. Cooling desserts to buy are peaches and cream or iced watermelon, and to quench warm-weather thirsts, lots of lemonade and iced tea are available. Bales of hay are arranged about the grounds so one can sit down on them, spread out his choice of eatables, and be comfortable while enjoying them.

All in all, there are about twenty-five food concessions at the fair. Youth, civic, and church groups are responsible for running most of them, and their profits help to support the activities of the various organizations through the year. Typical of these groups is the Mission City Cosmopolitan Club, whose booths serve daily, in two shifts of five couples each, both chalupas and chili con queso. Margie Sanchez, spokeswoman for the group, has supplied the recipes for both these specialties, and for those untutored in the refinements of chalupa-eating, she advises that at an outdoor function such as the Texas State Arts and Crafts Fair, these flat, crispy-fried and filled corn tortillas are eaten with the fingers and a napkin is kept close by. Chalupas, which in Mexico are little boats big enough for one or two persons, do look like crowded little boats filled with good things to eat. They are eaten with a knife and fork when served in a restaurant, but this isn't much easier than just biting into them sans tools. Regardless of eating approach, Mrs. Sanchez says of chalupas, "They're so good they're worth the trouble it takes to eat them." The chili con queso as served by the Mission City group is eaten in a like manner.

The entire fair setup is most pleasant to look upon. On the

tree-shaded lawns of Schreiner College in the center of Kerrville, gay red-and-white-striped tents are set up to house the exhibits of the fair. Through the grounds meanders a little brook in which children can wade. Inside the tents is a wide variety of contemporary, as well as pioneer, arts and crafts.

A few of the arts shown do have a relationship to food, although admittedly there are not many. A sourdough-bread maker allows one to relive the early days of the West, when pioneers depended on sourdough for their yeast breads, pancakes, and other life-sustaining breadstuffs. A more modern though completely decorative application of breadmaking is supplied by artists who fashion sculptures from bread dough which they bake and decorate to sell at the fair.

To get the feeling of photography's early days, you can have your tintype photo taken by one of the craftsmen specializing in this old-time art. If you yearn for a well-made and dependable slingshot, you can learn not only how to make your own but also how to shoot it safely. Spinning, dyeing, lye-soap making, horsehair-rope making, and blacksmithing are some of the other pioneer crafts demonstrated.

To rest the eye and give the ear a chance, a wide variety of musical entertainment is provided for everyone. Long-haired youths who come for the New Folk Concerts or the Folk Mass end up intrigued by the older, long-hair-pinned-up generation who demonstrate some of their old-time skills and play some of their old-time music. People of all ages enjoy the diversion of the Fiddler's Contest as well as the daily dance performances by the Hill Country Arts Foundation and Ballet Folkloric de San Antonio. Running more or less concurrently with the Texas State Arts and Crafts Fair is the Kerrville Folk Festival, providing evening musical entertainment.

The following recipes for Chalupas and Chili con Queso have been scaled down to family-size servings from fair-size cooking.

CHALUPAS

2 *one-pound cans refried beans*

1 *small bottle or can of beer*

1 *package of 12 precooked corn tortillas (or 1 ten-ounce can tortillas and vegetable oil for frying)*

$^1/_2$ *head lettuce, shredded*

2 *or 3 medium-sized tomatoes, chopped*

$^1/_4$ *pound Cheddar cheese, shredded*

1 *small can Mexican hot sauce or sauce for tacos (preferably containing little or no vinegar)*

Empty the refried beans into a saucepan and heat slowly, stirring often and thinning with the beer until the beans are the consistency of soft mashed potatoes.

Meanwhile, pour the vegetable oil into a skillet to a depth of $^1/_4$ to $^1/_2$ inch. Fry 12 tortillas quickly, 1 at a time, turning once, until crisp. Drain on paper towels. (Or have ready the pre-cooked tortillas.)

Spread the hot beans over the tortillas. Top with a mound of shredded lettuce, a tablespoon of chopped tomatoes, a spoonful of shredded Cheddar cheese, and Mexican hot sauce or sauce for tacos to taste.

MAKES 1 DOZEN

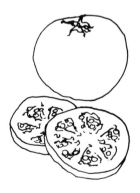

CHILI CON QUESO

1 *one-pound package Velveeta cheese*

$1/2$ *of a* $7^1/2$*-ounce can tomatoes with chilies (such as Rotel, Patio, or Old El Paso brands. The can may also be labeled "tomatoes and jalapeño peppers." If not available, use canned tomatoes and chopped jalapeño peppers.)*

$1/4$ *cup beer*

1 *tablespoon (or to taste) chopped jalapeño peppers, seeds removed*

1 *package of 12 precooked corn tortillas (or 1 ten-ounce can tortillas and vegetable oil for frying)*

In the top of a double boiler over hot water, melt the Velveeta cheese, stirring occasionally. When melted, add the tomatoes with chilies, beer, and chopped jalapeño peppers. Continue to heat while preparing the tortillas.

Pour the vegetable oil into a skillet to a depth of $1/4$ to $1/2$ inch. Fry 12 tortillas quickly, 1 at a time, turning once, until crisp. Drain on paper towels. (Or have ready the precooked tortillas.)

Spread the hot cheese mixture over the tortillas.

MAKES 1 DOZEN

Festival Facts

The Texas State Arts and Crafts Fair, which began in 1972, is held annually on Memorial Day weekend at the campus of Schreiner College in Kerrville, Texas, located on Highway 27, about seventy miles northwest of San Antonio, via Interstate 10. For further information, write: Texas State Arts and Crafts Fair, Box 12008, Capitol Station, Austin, Texas 78711.

Tucson Festival's Fiesta de la Placita and San Xavier Fiesta

35

Tucson, Arizona

Tucson, originally the site of an Indian village called Stjukshon, was settled in 1775 as a fortified town of the Spanish colonial empire, and now glories in its Indian, Spanish, Mexican, and pioneer heritage each year at the Tucson Festival, a three-week-long, many-faceted series of events. While it may be difficult for some to choose from among the many happenings, including the Arizona Watercolor Association Exhibit, Pioneer Days at Old Fort Lowell, the Fiesta de los Niños, and concerts by the Tucson Symphony Orchestra, from a food lover's point of view, the two "must" events are the Fiesta de la Placita and the San Xavier Fiesta.

The two-day-long Fiesta de la Placita is a merry Mexican street fair filled with bright paper flowers, music from mariachi bands, stands selling piñatas (gaily decorated papier-mâché animals and figures filled with toys and candies for the children) and other souvenirs, and from thirty to forty colorful puestos (booths) selling Mexican dishes, delicacies, refreshments, and treats by the dozens.

One particular fiesta specialty, a favorite of Tucsonites, is Green Corn Tamales. This dish, as well as Biscochuelos, rich orange- and anise-flavored cookie rings, are available at the puestos, and Mrs. Mary Rivera, a member of one of Tucson's old Mexican families, has kindly shared her recipes for both of them. When you make the tamales, it's a good idea to do them as a team effort, since they do take time to put together and are most fun done with a group.

Foods are relished, Mexican dancers applauded, musicians and singers hailed, and the queen of the fiesta cheered, all in acknowledgment of Cinco de Mayo, the celebration of a victory of the Mexican Republic over Emperor Maximilian, who tried to take over Mexico with a French army on May 5 (Cinco de Mayo), 1862.

"Dramatic" best describes an evening event of the Tucson Festival called the San Xavier Fiesta, on the San Xavier Papago Reservation. It commemorates the founding of, and takes place at, the Mission San Xavier del Bac—if not the most important building in the state of Arizona, then certainly the most famous and magnificent mission in the southern part of the state. The story of the mission is relived in a pageant replete with mounted Spanish soldiers, a procession lit by a hundred mesquite fires, tolling bells, and fireworks.

The Papago Indians, who take an active part in the pageant, also supply both contemporary and traditional Papago music and dancing. In one such dance, the Round Dance, spectators are invited to join in the simple steps that circle around Papago singers and basket drummers. All dances done by the Papagos and the Yaqui Indians during the San Xavier Fiesta are considered social dances, as opposed to more sacred and private dances which are not done before the public. They are all, regardless of category, ancient dances that have to do with nature, rain, the seasons of the year, harvests, aspects of life, and so forth. The Papagos, most of whom have been Christians since 1692 when the Jesuit missionary Father Eusebio Francisco Kino came to their village, quite easily maintain their Christian beliefs while carrying on the customs and traditions of their Indian culture.

Papago foods are served before the pageant and the entertainment is presented, and such dishes as Papago Chili and Papago Popovers are savored by all. Recipes for these specialties have been given to us by Frances Manuel of the Papago people of the desert region of Tucson.

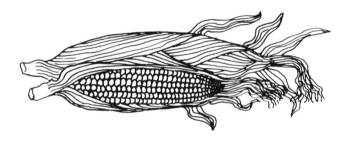

GREEN CORN TAMALES

1 *dozen ears white corn*
1 *pound lard*
1 *heaping tablespoon salt (or to taste)*
1 *pound cottage cheese*
2 *or 3 four-ounce cans green chilies*

Cut off the stems of the corn about $1/2$ inch past where the stem ends. Remove the husks and corn silk, discarding the silk. Trim the pointed ends off the husks. Wash the husks well in hot water and allow them to sit in hot water while proceeding with the recipe.

Grate the corn from the cobs. This is done most easily with a grater having round holes about $1/4$ inch in diameter. If you live in an area where there are places that process Mexican food, take the grated corn there to have it ground very fine. Otherwise, put the corn through a food processor, half at a time, or through a blender, a small amount at a time.

Line the bottom of a large steamer pot with the corncobs.

Cream the lard with an electric mixer until fluffy. Add the grated corn and mix until well blended. Add the salt and mix well. Add the cottage cheese and blend until fluffy.

Remove the seeds from the green chilies. Cut them into long strips, or dice them.

Drain the cornhusks well. Using the best husks and reserving all others for lining the cooking pot and for tearing into tying strips, proceed to stuff the husks. Spread a heaping tablespoon of filling lengthwise on the husk. Add a teaspoonful or 2 long strips of the green chilies. Fold the sides of the husk one over the other to conceal the filling. Fold up the pointed end of the husk about 3 inches. Fold the broad end down over it. With a narrow strip of husk, tie up the tamale around the top flap. (This may be a little difficult to do at first, but you will get the knack of it soon and will be able to tie them without breaking the narrow strip.)

When all the tamales are assembled, line the bottom and sides of the pot with the remaining husks. Add enough water to come just to the top of the husks. Arrange the tamales in the lined pot by stacking upright, broad, tied end *up*, somewhat in the style of a Halloween corn shock. They should be packed quite firmly. If there are any cornhusks left over, cover the top of the tamales with them. Place a tight-fitting lid on the pot. Bring to a boil, reduce the heat, and steam for 1 hour.

If not eaten immediately, the tamales can be wrapped in foil and frozen. To reheat, bake in a preheated 350° oven for 30 minutes.

MAKES ABOUT 75

BISCOCHUELOS

1 pound lard
1¹/₂ cups sugar
4 egg yolks

$^3/_4$ *teaspoon salt*
$^3/_4$ *cup masa harina (Quaker Oats brand is available in groceries in the West and in Spanish grocery stores in other parts of the United States)*
1 *tablespoon anise seeds*
6 *cups flour*
1 *cup plus* 2 *tablespoons orange juice (fresh or canned unsweetened)*

Beat the lard with an electric mixer until fluffy. Add the sugar gradually and continue beating. Add the egg yolks and combine well. Add the salt, masa harina, and anise seeds, and mix well. Add the flour and orange juice alternately, mixing well after each addition. Cover and refrigerate 8 hours or overnight.

Preheat the oven at 350°. Take small pieces of the dough and with the palms of the hands roll them back and forth on a lightly floured board to form pencil-thin rolls of dough. Cut or pinch off 6-inch lengths, and form the dough into rings. Arrange on ungreased baking sheets. Bake 10 to 12 minutes until lightly browned at the edges.

MAKES ABOUT 10 DOZEN

PAPAGO CHILI

3 *pounds chuck, cut into chunks*
2$^1/_2$ *cups dried red chilies*
$^1/_2$ *cup shortening*
2 *garlic cloves, crushed*
1 *teaspoon salt*

Simmer the chuck in boiling salted water, just to cover, for 1$^1/_2$ to 2 hours, or until tender. Remove from the heat, remove the meat from the liquid, and when cool enough to handle, shred the meat, discarding any fat or gristle.

Meanwhile, cut open the chilies and remove and discard the seeds. Scatter the chilies on a baking sheet and roast about 10 minutes in a 275° oven, making certain the chilies do not scorch. Remove from the oven and place in a bowl. Cover with cold water and soak 1 hour. Drain the chilies.

In a heavy saucepan, melt the shortening. Add the garlic, salt, and drained chilies and bring to a simmer. Cook over the lowest flame, covered, for 1 hour, stirring often. Add the shredded meat, mix well, and continue cooking for 30 minutes.

Serve with Papago Popovers or tortillas, or use as a sandwich filling or as a filling for burritos (wheat-flour tacos). To use as a main dish, serve with beans and a salad.

MAKES 10 OR MORE SERVINGS. THE RECIPE MAY BE DOUBLED.

PAPAGO POPOVERS

2 cups fresh milk, sour milk, or evaporated milk
1 teaspoon salt
5 cups flour (more or less, depending on the kind of milk used)
10 teaspoons baking powder (or 2 teaspoons for each cup of flour used)
Fat for frying

Combine the milk and salt, and add enough flour to make a smooth bread dough—about 5 cups of flour if you are using fresh milk. Work the dough, pulling with the fingers, until it is stretchy. Then add the baking powder, blending it in with a spoon or with the hands. With floured hands form the dough into egg-sized balls and set on a tray lined with waxed paper or plastic wrap.

Heat the fat until hot but not smoking. Take one dough ball at a time and stretch the dough into as large a circle as possible—as near the size of a plate as you can stretch it. The first few may be difficult to shape, but you will soon get the knack of how to pull the dough. Fry, one at a time, until brown on one side; then turn and brown the other side. Drain on paper towels. Continue until all the dough balls have been stretched and fried.

Serve with Papago Chili, or with honey, or plain.

MAKES ABOUT 2 DOZEN

Festival Facts

The Tucson Festival is held annually from mid-April to mid-May. It was organized by the Tucson Festival Society in 1950, and some of the many events include the Fiesta de la Placita, Tucson Community Center Plaza, Church Avenue opposite St. Augustine Cathedral, Tucson, Arizona, and the San Xavier Fiesta, San Xavier del Bac Mission, San Xavier Papago Indian Reservation, Tucson, Arizona, reached by the South Sixth Avenue Extension in the southwestern section of the city. For further information, write: Tucson Festival Society, 8 West Paseo Redondo, Tucson, Arizona 85705.

Vermont's Northeast Kingdom Annual Fall Foliage Festival

36

Six Towns in Northeastern Vermont

The air is crisp, the stars shine bright in the clear night sky, you're comfortably filled with the sturdy foods of a New England church supper, the sound of a rousing march played by the St. Johnsbury Band comes from the windows of Peacham's town hall, and life seems suddenly uncomplicated, peaceful, and good. And with this feeling, the goal of the northeastern Vermonters has been achieved, for they want to show during their festival days how they live all year round, the simple things they eat and do that bring them enjoyment, and the activities peculiar to Vermont.

Whether one stays for one day of the festival in one town, or moves on to enjoy the next day in the next town, or even decides to stay on for six days and visit all six towns, one gets on intimate terms with life and people in the tucked-away villages that participate in the annual festival. What began as a weekend event in the town of Danville in 1956, two years later turned into a six-town event, with each town having its own day of activities. Walden, Cabot, Plainfield, Marshfield, Peacham, Barnet Center, and Groton, all between fifty and seventy-five miles south of the Canadian border, are the towns that generally take part, and in October all are set in the blazing glory of autumn foliage that makes picture postcards look pale by comparison.

A special part of each day's event is a foliage tour conducted in an easy and comfortable way. You drive your own car, and a guide leads each small entourage of automobiles through back roads, past small houses and farms, rolling hills, and mountains all splendid in dazzling autumn dress. The tours stop for especially lovely views, for picture taking, and for just letting one be close enough to the leaves to touch them and marvel at their colors and perhaps pick up an especially pretty one to take home as a remembrance.

Some towns have their own special tours in addition, with Walden, for instance, adding a farm tour and stops at a country school and a small, family-operated sawmill. Those interested in old gravestones are invited to visit one of the small cemeteries not uncommon in the area to examine some of the markings. Cabot includes hiking tours, shutterbug tours, and a visit to their local creamery, where milk is brought in to be pasteurized and made into cottage cheese, yogurt, butter, and the famous Vermont Cheddar, which is referred to locally simply as "cheese." Tours from Peacham, a historic town settled in 1776, include a village tour with a stop at the Historical Association House. Barnet Center's tours feature old homes, with Goodwillie House being one of the more outstanding. Built in 1791 and occupied by the town's first minister and his wife, and then by their son, who was also a minister, for a total of eighty years, the house was once a station of the Underground Railroad, and one can still see the place where the runaway slaves took refuge in the basement of the house on their flight to Canada and freedom.

Festival breakfasts, lunches, and suppers are served in nearly every town, and since so many of the people's social activities center around the town churches, most of the festival meals are served there. In Groton a lusty Lumberjack Breakfast starts off the day's activities. While the area's former lumber-camp days are over, the kind of breakfast the lumberjacks once ate reappears during festival time, with fruit juice, oatmeal, ham, sausage, pancakes with Vermont maple syrup, hashed-brown potatoes liberally sprinkled with paprika before being fried in bacon fat, doughnuts, pies, and coffee offering a challenge to the most ravenous appetite. Other towns have coffee hours or serve less ambitious breakfasts, such as Barnet Center, where sausages made at Kimball and Miles, the local general store, are featured with the pancakes and maple syrup, doughnuts, rolls, muffins, and coffee, and all at the most modest prices.

Lunches are light and usually feature sandwiches and homemade pies, with Peacham throwing in a special sugar-on-snow treat (Vermont maple syrup on shaved ice, real snow not yet having fallen), and Cabot serving a hot beef stew. A few towns also serve afternoon tea to provide a few moments for foot resting.

At dinnertime the simple, good-tasting, piping-hot New England specialties are served at two or three sittings to accommodate all the appetites built up by afternoon outings in the invigorating fall air. Typical of such dinners is one recently served to three hundred visitors at Peacham, where the long tables seating ten persons each were decorated with driftwood centerpieces gathered at Peacham Pond by a young townswoman who trimmed them with autumnal touches to provide a background for Vermont baked beans, vegetable hash, frankfurters, brown bread, cabbage salad, lengthwise-cut, peeled cucumber pickles, and other accompaniments which preceded a staggering selection of homemade pies, coffee, and tea. Originally serving only apple and pumpkin, the pie-making ladies have branched out to include in their repertoire mince, raspberry, cherry, maple, lemon, rhubarb, and chocolate, to name but a few.

To an outsider the two most interesting dishes are the Vegetable Hash and the Vermont Baked Beans. The Vegetable Hash, as explained by Peacham's Ruby Goslant, is, in a sense, a ground-up version of a New England boiled dinner, since it contains all the ingredients of such a meal (with a little less meat), but is ground up and served as a vegetable dish instead of leaving each vegetable and the meat whole. Mrs. Goslant, who has been active with Peacham's church supper for a dozen or more years, has provided instructions (below) for making the Vegetable Hash, but points out that the quantities of each vegetable used are the prerogative of the maker.

What makes the baked beans of northeastern Vermont different from others is the choice of beans used. Local people swear by soldier beans, which are a little smaller than kidney beans but similarly shaped and white in color with a small streak of red on the inner side. Another local favorite is the yellow eye bean, a little smaller than the soldier bean and yellow in color. Some people raise the beans in their own gardens, but they are also readily available in local stores and markets. Each person has her own favorite method of preparing the beans, but typical and delicious is Francese Cochran's recipe (below), as served at the Walden Hot Dish Supper. Other dishes generally served at Walden's supper are either chicken and biscuits or meat loaf, old-fashioned macaroni and cheese, red flannel or red beet hash, the ubiquitous cabbage salad, homemade pickles, fall vegetables, and applesauce and cupcakes for dessert. Plainfield features a pot roast of beef dinner with hot johnny cake, Cabot a turkey supper, and Barnet Center a buffet-style dinner of ham baked with maple syrup, baked potatoes, buttered yellow squash, Harvard beets, green beans, cabbage salad, banana-nut bread, and chocolate, white, and maple cakes. Six churches work together to produce the supper, dividing the work into baking and vegetable-preparing teams.

A tradition of most of the towns is to hold an old-time hymn-sing either before supper, when people are waiting for their particular seating times, or as an evening entertainment. Favorite numbers are played by request (one simply calls out a number from the hymn book), and it's easy to get into the spirit of things with a singing of "O Beautiful for Spacious Skies" or "Faith of Our Fathers." For those who prefer to listen and watch rather than participate, other simple but appropriate entertainment is provided in the form of music, films, and Vermont poetry reading. One of the noteworthy evening entertainments is a concert by the St. Johnsbury Band, the third-oldest band in America (the Allentown Pennsylvania Band being the oldest, and the U.S. Military Academy Band the next oldest), which is composed of both sexes in every age group from teenagers to those in their seventies.

Daytime activities, in addition to touring and eating, include such things as a demonstration of Christmas-wreath making, using native balsam trimmed with pinecones and red bows, by Ethel Hatch at the Walden event. Mrs. Hatch shows how you can make your own wreath and also takes orders to make them for you, sometimes turning out as many as 250 wreaths in a season. Arts and crafts of all kinds are displayed in every town, and bazaars offer old books, baked goods, secondhand items, cider made on the spot in hand-operated presses, a display of antique safes, and other diversions.

Probably because it has the Saturday time slot of the festival, Groton attracts the largest crowd on its day. The long-established Chicken Pie Supper attracts regulars who meet there to catch up on the past year's events, and an afternoon parade appeals to young visitors as much as the evening no-dress-up Lumberjack Ball appeals to the adults.

People from thirty or more states and from other nations who visit the Fall Foliage Festival each year often return in following years to enjoy once again the beauty of Vermont's byroads and the hospitality of its villages that make such visits memorable.

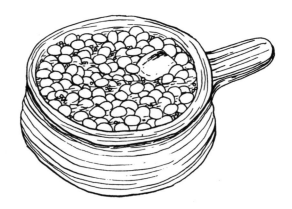

VEGETABLE HASH

1 *bunch beets*
1 *small yellow turnip (rutabaga)*
4 *large potatoes, peeled and halved*
2 *large onions, peeled and cut into chunks*
1 *bunch carrots, scraped and cut into 1- or 2-inch pieces*
1 *small cabbage, core removed, and cut into chunks*
$^1/_2$ *pound (amount is optional) cooked corned beef or ham, cut into chunks*

Cook the beets in boiling water, peel, and cut into chunks, discarding the cooking water.

Meanwhile, peel the turnip, cut it into chunks, and begin cooking it in a large pot with boiling water to cover well. After 15 minutes add the potatoes, onions, carrots, and cabbage, and continue cooking, adding more boiling water if necessary, until all vegetables are tender. Drain, reserving a few cups of the vegetable cooking water.

Put the beets and all other vegetables through a meat grinder with the corned beef or ham. Put back into the large pot. Add a cup of the cooking liquid and heat the mixture, stirring often, until piping hot, adding more of the liquid if necessary to prevent scorching. Serve as a vegetable.

MAKES 16 OR MORE SERVINGS

VERMONT BAKED BEANS

> 2 *pounds dried beans, preferably soldier beans or yellow eye beans,*
>   *but if not available use navy (pea) beans or similar beans*
> $^1/_2$ *teaspoon baking soda*
> $^1/_2$ *teaspoon salt*
> *Dash of pepper*
> 1 *cup brown sugar, maple sugar, or white sugar, or a combination*
>   *of any of the three*
> 1 *teaspoon dry mustard*
> $^1/_2$ *teaspoon ginger*
> $^1/_4$ *cup molasses*
> $^1/_2$ *pound (amount optional) salt pork, scored or cut up*

Pick over the beans and soak them overnight in cold water to cover by several inches. Transfer the beans and water to a pot, add the baking soda, and bring to a boil. Lower the heat and simmer about 30 minutes, until beans are slightly soft. Drain. Rinse in cold water.

Preheat the oven at 300°. Transfer the beans to a bean pot or similar-type casserole, or covered baking pot. Add the remaining ingredients. Add boiling water to come just below the top of the beans. Cover and bake 4 to 5 hours, checking the beans occasionally to see that the water level is maintained, adding boiling water if necessary, and now and then gently spooning beans from the bottom of the pot to the top so they cook evenly. During the last hour of baking, remove the lid.

NOTE: Long, slow cooking makes the best-flavored baked beans. If desired, a cut-up onion can be buried in the beans before baking.

MAKES ABOUT 10 SERVINGS

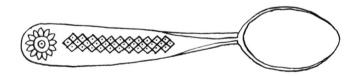

Festival Facts

Vermont's Northeast Kingdom Annual Fall Foliage Festival, which began in 1958, is held for six days, Monday through Saturday, in late September and/or early October. Each of six towns holds a festival for one day, and the towns include six of the following: Walden, Cabot, Plainfield, Peacham, Barnet Center, Groton, Marshfield, and sometimes Danville, Passumpsic, and Ryegate. These towns may be reached on local roads off U.S. 2 or U.S. 5 (Interstate 91). For further information, write: Fall Festival Committee, Box 38, West Danville, Vermont 05873.

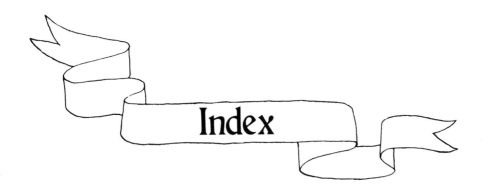

Index

269